ACCO...

UNREQUESTED BLESSINGS

"What if the greatest challenge in your life became the gateway to Heaven's glory? Here is a story not to be missed, of a little girl born with unforeseen obstacles, of a family's irrepressible love, and ultimately, of the Father's unsurpassed goodness. Your faith will be stretched and your heart freshly inspired as the Lord's kindness is revealed through Unrequested Blessings."

–Emily Tomko, author of *The Two Kingdoms: Understanding Your Role in Spiritual Warfare*

"I have seen first-hand the fruitfulness of Molly's life and am convinced that her message of simple trust and simple worship will continue to make an impact in significant ways in the months and years to come.".

–P.C. Alexander, Director PTL-India

"Volumes have been written; debates have raged on the meaning of life. But when a father comes face-to-face with the reality of caring for his severely challenged daughter, life is redefined. Written with honesty and interspersed with humor, Don Hess, pens his journey into the discovery of the beauty, power, and purpose of the physically challenged child. Caregivers, parents, and

healthcare workers alike will find this readable, moving narrative hard to put down."

–Sue Kawase, RN, retired teacher, and Molly's aunt

"Molly is a child born in due season who God used to bring great bonding and love to her family, and great blessings to the body of Christ. Through her life we see the great presence of The Lord even in quietness. Her life of worship as described in this book teaches us that worship is a spiritual connection with God. In writing the book Unrequested Blessings, her parents take us through a journey of Love, faith, total dependence on God, and a willingness to answer the call of ministry of faithfulness in caring for Molly until her mission on earth is fulfilled. As you read this book and feel the impact of Molly's earthly ministry, may God help you to realize your calling in life."

–Chinedum & Nkechi Uwaga, Co-founders of We Impact Africa, author of *Ask: And It Will Be Given to You*

"What an honor it was to stand on the platform with Molly Hess in India. What a joy to see the pastors of the region standing together in worship, in prayer, joining hands on behalf of our nation."

–Bonny Andrews, LiveJam founder

THE MOLLY HESS STORY

UNREQUESTED
BLESSINGS

Defining faith and the goodness of God

DON HESS

HigherLife Development Services, Inc.
P.O. Box 623307
Oviedo, Florida 32762
(407) 563-4806
www.ahigherlife.com

Printed in Canada
10 9 8 7 6 5 4 3 2 1   25 26 24 23 22 21 20 19

The Library of Congress has catalogued Unrequested Blessings as follows:

Hess, Don
Unrequested Blessings
ISBN: 978-1-951492-88-5

NOTE OF THANKS

There are many people to thank, and if you are reading this book and you had any part, large or small, in the life of Molly Hess, we as a family are deeply indebted to you and offer a heartfelt thank you.

A special thanks to our friend and author, Emily Tomko, for tireless hours of helping edit the book and for your encouragement to publish beyond family and friends.

Thank you HigherLife Publishing for your professional and valued service.

Thank you Nicole C. Mullen, Karen Brockington, and team for allowing Molly's love for your music to open up new worlds of opportunity for others.

Thank you to our parents, our siblings, and families, all the agencies of care, and The Worship Center and LifeGate church families for loving and believing in Molly.

DEDICATION

To our children Joseph, Kalah, Emily, and Matthew: These stories were written for your remembrance. Thank you for allowing God to shape, mold, and define you through one who never walked, talked, or spoke a word. You loved your sister Molly regardless of what she could not do. You valued her despite our not understanding fully. You came to trust God each in your own way and for this there is no greater joy. Your mother and I will be forever grateful. I am so very proud of each of you.

To their spouses Angela, Matt, Seth, and Carissa: Thank you for saying "yes" to our children and for also sharing in this journey of love and understanding Molly. Thank you for joining our family. We hold in our hearts deep gratitude for each one of you. Thank you for accepting and valuing Molly. I believe your marriages will be better because of Molly. She defined who we are and how we view others. She taught us to be aware of others before ourselves.

See to it that the stories of Molly are passed on to your children and to your children's children.

To my wife, Kathy: You are my hero. Though you counted yourself unworthy and unprepared to care for Molly, you allowed the God who gives to provide what you needed. You lived your struggles like an open book for many to see and learn. Thank you for allowing me to share Molly's story with those beyond our knowing. There is no story without you. You passed the greatest of tests. You loved in word and deed when word and deed could not be reciprocated.

To Molly: I miss you. Thank you for your life. Thank you for your love. Thank you for your smiles.

TABLE OF CONTENTS

FOREWORD

This is a wonderful book. I wept and rejoiced my way through this book.

This book is about how the "word of faith" and the "word of practical reality" meet and enrich one another. It's about a mother's love and a father's love, each experienced and expressed in differing ways, that led to a richer family life instead of causing deep alienating conflicts.

This is not a theology text but the writer wrestles with theological issues at a deep level and he never lets go of God. And thus he receives the touch of the Father and the reassuring words, "You have wrestled with the God of Jacob, and your victory will bless the nations."

Read this book and be changed.

Dr. E. Daniel Martin

CHAPTER 1

HER NAME WAS MOLLY

It was two thirty in the afternoon on Friday, August 3, 2018. I was by my daughter Molly's bedside. Molly was her usual silent self and lying in a sixth floor ICU hospital bed. The bed was slightly elevated and across her legs lay the double blankets her nurses had placed there. Her eyes were closed, as if resting. Her normally thin beautiful face was now swollen, the result of failing kidneys; her breathing, though steady, was controlled by the ventilator.

I dozed off for about ten minutes then woke quickly, still somewhat foggy, to a young girl's voice.

"I am going to remember this day for as long as I live."

Wondering where the voice had come from, I glanced around the room, only to find that Molly and I were alone. Next my gaze fell on the iPad, which had been playing nonstop music. I picked it up and scrolled through the last few songs in case the words were penned in one of the songs' lyrics, but there seemed to be no connection.

The sound of the voice I heard was like the one I could have only imagined Molly's might have sounded. It was a carefree, happy, lively, joy-filled voice that exuded no sound of pain or discomfort.

The fogginess of slumber now gone, I knew with certainty this was Molly's voice. There was no other explanation. Molly and Jesus were having their conversation. Her course was set.

Jesus had come.

Heaven was calling.

Heaven was waiting.

Molly was set free from pain that Friday. This is my absolute belief. And in the early morning hours of Monday, August 6, her heart on this earth stopped beating.

She was twenty-four years and eight months old.

It was as I crawled into bed a few weeks later that the realization finally hit me: her memories and her pictures were all we had left. It was too much to bear. I could still feel her hair and sense the softness of her smooth cheeks. But she was not there. She was not there to tuck in. She was not there to give us her bedtime smile.

I struggled to hang on to the memory of her words and voice.

"I am going to remember this day for as long as I live."

Heaves of emotion issued forth from deep within me. Hers was a voice I wanted to treasure forever, but I knew as time went by the memory would fade. I wept because I did not understand why I got to hear her voice when no one else did. I wept because I wanted her brothers and sisters, and her mother, Kathy, who cared for her all these years, to hear her voice too.

For twenty-four plus years we carried, tarried, and were married to the task of caring for Molly. We loved Molly despite the fact that she never walked or talked. We loved her though she never spoke a word.

At Molly's memorial service, her oldest brother Joseph would say what we all felt.

I feel totally inadequate to the task of finding words that would do justice to Molly's life. Attempting to appropriately describe what the person who represented so much of what was beautiful and so much of what was painful about life meant to me and to our family is a task that's simply impossible. There are so many things about her life that we probably won't know until we get to heaven, so instead of speculating about answers I don't have, this I know for certain: Molly defined our family.

CHAPTER 2

WINKIN', BLINKIN', AND A NOD

My wife, Kathy, and I have found ourselves thankful time and again for our strong Christian heritage. A house built on a rock will stand against the pending storms of life, and without our faith-filled upbringing, life might have been quite different. Our parents provided us a solid foundation of simple faith.

Ours were homes where God was honored, and the Bible was not just a book on a shelf. Rather, it was read and believed. There were the typical religious do's and don'ts within both our tight-knit communities, as in don't drink, smoke, chew tobacco...or hang out with people that do. Church was an active part of our lives.

My dad was a farmer; my mother was raised a town girl. Joe and Lois Hess had seven children in their first ten years, and that will make most parents call upon Jesus, and my parents did just that. After a gap of almost four years, I came along. They thought they were done and named me Don for short. A great surprise came five years later in my little brother Dan. They now had three and a half dozen as my dad would fondly say with a twinkle in his eyes.

Kathy's father was a self-employed equipment operator and also a pastor for twenty-five years, and her mother was graced with a caring pastoral heart as well. Kathy was the second of four children to Harold and Alma Shultz.

When Kathy was thirteen, her family answered the call to relocate from quaint Lancaster County, Pennsylvania, to rural LeRoy, Minnesota, to help pastor the new families there that had recently sold everything back East and bought cheaper farmland in the West.

Painfully shy before she went, she was even more so in this new environment. Kathy could barely speak in front of others. But reading a book about the two types of pride changed her dramatically. The more common boastful pride is being proud of one's own self. The other less common form is worm pride. This is being comfortable in the devaluing of one's own self despite what God sees them as. It was an awakened moment to her spirit when she realized her shyness was pride because her fear of what others thought did not value who God made her to be. By the time she returned two-and-a-half-years later to Lancaster, Pennsylvania, to finish high school, others were asking what happened to this shy, bashful young girl.

Of course, meeting a charming and handsome-by-his-mother'sstandards young boy named Donnie, I would like to think assisted this newfound joy and confidence. Kathy had returned to Lancaster and spent ninth grade at her local public school before she transferred to Lancaster Mennonite School for grades ten through twelve, at the same time I did.

My embellished version of our first acquaintance and interaction is that she winked at me. It was the start of a morning tenth grade gym class, and most of the class had changed into their gym clothes and were out on the gym floor preparing for the morning activities. To this day I remember the exact spot on the gym floor; it was the east side of the gym just off-center of the basketball hoop. There was a group of four or five girls sitting in a circle and stretching as I strode by rather slowly and in stud-like fashion.

She caught my attention with those big beautiful eyes as she looked up at me and said, "You had a good game last night!"

Her version of when we first locked eyes is a tad different. She remembers complimenting me on my JV basketball game, which had taken place the evening prior, but certainly there was no wink. At best, it could have been a blink, but even so, surely of the non-flirtatious courting sort. Regardless of whose version is true, truly I was smitten like a kitten that a girl would talk to a somewhat backward farm boy like me, and whether it was a wink or a blink, what did sink in was her deep set of sparkling eyes that seemed to make my heart skip a beat and go flitter-flutter. It was physical education at its best.

This all took place despite the fact that the girl's required attire in gym class was a putridly striped yellow (and pardon the farmer-ish description, but it looked like the color of newborn calf poop). Yes, it was that ugly. The emotional scars of the required (but now retired) attire are evidenced by the ban put on bringing old yearbooks to our Class of 1981 reunions for fear of any gym class pictures reappearing.

The attire may have been ugly, but Kathy Shultz was not. She radiated a sense of God's grace and beauty to me and to others. She was popular with the popular and the not-so-popular. She was serious about caring and valuing others, all fed by her newfound faith in knowing God valued her, and she did not have to be shy about it. Her noticeable alluring physical and inner beauty made her quite a catch.

As a mere sixteen-year-old tenth grader, I found myself dreaming and scheming about how best to make my move. My dad was fondly referred to as "Unslow Joe" for his hurried approach to work and play, but I humbly confess his giddy-up-and-go anointing simply giddied-up-and-went when it came to me in this situation. It took me nearly twelve months to get up the courage to ask Kathy out on a date.

But the courage eventually came thanks to a go-between mediator and classmate named Twila. She made sure Kathy would say "yes" when the time came, which was a late December Thursday night at our local roller-skating rink called Overlook. The plan was in place, and the assurance was in place that my heartthrob would be there. Most importantly, it was all but sewed up that she would give me the affirmative wink if I asked her out.

Quite vivid is the memory, and no, the plan was not to wait for the last song of the evening. It's just that farmer Don needed time to calm his nerves and gather his composure. This was a big deal. The last song of the night came on; the lights went dim; the music was romantically in sync with the moment, and we were holding hands as we circled the rink. Scared spit-less and speechless, my mouth was dry. Try as I might, no words would come. Terror was setting in as the song and music were coming to an end. The dimmed lights now gradually were fading back on. I reached down deep and desperately voiced forth some sort of mumble-jumble about inviting her out on a date.

Anxiously I awaited her response. I waited some more. And then some more. She finally turned and looked at me with a somewhat perplexed look and said clearly, "Did you say something?" My heart sank like a tank, but thankfully, I recomposed my voice and now with the music completely faded and the lights back on, she either heard me or more-than-likely just read my stammering lips, and she said "yes."

Oh yeah! And I've been smiling ever since.

We dated through the rest of our junior and senior years of high school. Three months after graduation I went off to a five-month stint of Bible school and mission work with a Youth Evangelism Service team from our church who worked in conjunction with an organization called Youth With A Mission (YWAM). It was life changing, and I liked it so much that I convinced Kathy to go. And she did. We wrote lots of letters back and forth and signed them with "your brother (or sister) in the Lord." Our children found copies years later and seemed to think that was quite a hoot.

Upon her return to Pennsylvania, Kathy was contemplating a two-year Bible school, and I thought I had better make my move regarding spending our lives together. Thankfully, she said "yes" (and this time with more than a wink), and six months later, on December 31, 1983, we were married. We were both just twenty years old, but by our own self-proclaimed judgment, a very mature twenty.

Our similar family and church backgrounds and YWAM experiences would lend themselves to help us when challenges eventually came. It would take a special person a mere ten years later to care for and love this little girl named Molly. And Kathy was chosen.

Little did we know how Molly would one day define and refine our family.

CHAPTER 3

A CHORD NOT BROKEN

During her fourth pregnancy, Kathy would comment that there were some ever-so-slight indications that things were different. There were the usual sonograms, but they showed nothing conclusive. These sonograms did leave the door open for more tests to search for potential developmental issues or other problems; however, these, they said, would only give us information in case we wanted the option of early termination of the child. We would have never considered termination based on our biblical understanding and strong belief that life begins at conception and chose not to have additional tests. Kathy would drop a comment now and then as in, "The baby is not very active" or "This go-round feels different."

In the midst of the busyness of life with six-year-old Joseph, four-year-old Kalah, and two-year-old Emily, I was running my own drywall business, and the extra expense and time for doctor visits was not the forefront of my focus. I have since forgiven myself for the sin of presumption, but I based my routine on a healthy dose of positive theology that did not waste much time on what could go wrong. By nature I never took "what ifs" too seriously. Maybe my being the eighth child, and always having food on the table, I just was not the worrying sort. I am a healthy "Seven" on the Enneagram charts, a golden retriever on the four personality types, and a solid "S" on the DISC profile. I'm a good-natured, positive, steady-Eddie.

Kathy seemed to have a deep sense of calling to motherhood, and with the first three children being rather easy deliveries, the assumption was that this fourth delivery would be no different. All was going along quite handsomely according to our verbally agreed upon dreams and desire to have a family with five children.

We would surmise, looking back, that Molly most likely had some developmental issues in the womb. Added to those issues were birth complications. Kathy's water broke during the early morning hours of December 18, 1993. The midwife arrived quickly to assist the home birth. But a cord prolapse ensued and nixed the home birth plan, so instead it was a harried ten minute high-speed dash to the local hospital at five thirty in the morning with the midwife and her aid monitoring Kathy in the back seat. There was a subsequent race against time to get personnel in place once at the hospital for an emergency C-section.

The exact doctors with experience in this type of crisis just happened be on the floor from a prior delivery during the third watch of the night, and this minimized the potential for even greater loss and perhaps even death of our baby.

Molly Elizabeth Hess was brought into this world without a whimper. Her Apgar score was "0-3." Our baby was whisked out of the womb and out of the room away from her mother to be resuscitated, revived, and connected to life support. She survived the day and the night, day two also, and by day three she was beginning to breathe on her own.

By day four, brain activity tests read by the neurologists painted a very bleak picture. Molly had taken quite a hit to the brain, more than likely due to the cord prolapse, which causes a loss of oxygen. The neurologist did not pull any punches. In fact, he seemed quite bent on making us feel like our mentioned hope in God was never going to be enough. He and his team of interns gave the option of inserting a feeding tube directly into her stomach, so she could be tube-fed since she could not eat through her mouth. This would most likely keep her alive, but it came with the stern warning that she would never function normally. Her brain issues were serious. Just how serious was yet to be determined.

The other option, an intern was asked to explain, was that, basically, we had the right to do nothing. We could simply let her die of hunger. I was appalled, shocked, and quite sickened by the audacity and gall of the medical team to suggest such an act. It caused a strong reaction, a disdain, a righteous indignation to rise up within me that would actually prove to be quite helpful in the weeks and years to come.

Years later, I would come across an article regarding hospitals reviewing their approach to certain psychological scare techniques. Their intent was to lay out the worst-case scenarios to the parents without presenting much if any hope while monitoring the parents' response. Parental reaction was to help them determine how aggressively to pursue full manner of care. The parents who fight back present a better case for the medical staff to proceed aggressively to save the child.

I like to think the neurology team was choosing this latter approach. This was clear: Molly would need a lot of folks to fight for her. It was eight weeks of touch-and-go, as Molly did not show many signs of normal development. There was no suck reflex, so we chose the G-tube route to feed her directly into the stomach.

Many friends and family were of great help and support those first weeks. In early February of 1994, Molly finally came home. She was greeted with her very own huge "Welcome Home" banner made by friends and hung with lots of love right above our garage-door entrance.

During Molly's first four months, she showed little outward expression. There was just a lonely, empty, blank stare. Her eyes were void of life. She did show an aversion to touch evidenced by a wince but other than that, she was generally emotionless.

For Kathy and I, like a blur, life moved on. Daily was the routine of my going to work and Kathy caring for the needs of not just Molly but the three other children. Try as she may to give them her full attention, she would be interrupted every two hours to stop everything to feed Molly. This was done by filling a large syringe with formula then patiently holding up the filled container to allow gravity to do its thing. It was an ever-so-slow wait for the liquid to drip drop into her stomach. This was done five times a day with no response from Molly signaling whether she was either satisfied or unsatisfied. The emotional toll of her silence and non-expressiveness was like warfare arrows poisoned with despair. Compounding this was the scurry of agency activity associated with trying to diagnose and label the yet-to-be-discovered extent of Molly's issues. The eventual fit-all label was cerebral palsy.

But our steadfast belief from the day she was born was that surely God would heal our daughter. It was a surprise it had not yet happened. Our faith, our confession of God being a good God, and our belief in the miraculous kept us going.

Molly was beginning to define our faith.

Molly (3 months)

17

CHAPTER 4

SIFTED SAINTS

It was a typical start to the week in Living Word Academy's elementary classroom. The teacher would ask the students to gather around for their weekly morning prayer time, and each child was asked to bring a prayer request. For Molly's older sister Kalah, it was a struggle to come up with a valid prayer need. She would try so hard to conjure up a request. In her mind, she and her family had no needs.

This we learned after-the-fact from her teacher during one of the annual parent-teacher conferences. It made quite an impression on the teacher that one could have a younger sister with special needs, and yet Kalah could not think of any prayer request. Not one. Early on, it seemed that God was gifting our young children with a special grace for Molly.

Some of this family-willed directive to see Molly as normal despite her physically not fitting the part came while Molly was still in the womb. It was October of 1993, Kathy was then seven months pregnant, and a young minister born in Pakistan and Bible-schooled in Sweden, traveled to America for a three-day conference at our church. Christopher Alam was preaching on healing and the baptisms of fire and the Holy Spirit. At the end of the service he called people forward for special prayer. Kathy had discovered at a recent doctor visit that the baby had turned and was in a breech position, so she went forward to ask for prayer. In the midst of praying over the crowd now gathered at the front, the minister abruptly turned from across the other side of the large platform, walked down the steps, and now standing right in front of Kathy, he pointed at her belly.

"The baby will be normal," he said.

After moving on to pray for others, he returned a second time and said again, only this time louder, "The baby will be normal!"

His tone was laced with emphatic importance. The Lord seemed to want to extenuate and emphasize the message to us. The message got to us; it was not forgotten. Heaven made sure.

However, our filters of thought and scope of understanding at the time caused only a slight pause of momentary perplexity, and neither of us deemed it to be that memorable or impactful. We assumed, presumptuously, that the baby would turn from this breech position and life would continue on its honkey-dory way. After all, life was good because God was good. It's what we declared out loud every Sunday and each day in between with words or song. I was married to my tenth-grade heartthrob; we had three healthy wonderful children; we had our own business that was surely blessed because we believed in tithing... Yes, one could almost see the storm clouds of sifting shifting in our direction.

The minister's message "the baby will be normal" would return to us many times in the early years, and even though our sights were on Molly's physical healing, his prophetic words helped us look at Molly as whole in most every other aspect. We chose to treat her as if she could hear and understand us perfectly, and we chose to assume she had feelings and emotions like the rest of us.

Void of expressiveness for the first four months, a day came when Molly gave us an ever-so-slight smile. It was one happy and memorable day. Neurologically, there was slow development, and then slight but unusual movements emerged. With mild smiled expressions came slightly discomforted expressions and with her first sounds came pained sounds which gave way to eventual loud, shrill, untimely screams. These sudden shrieks started coming most every night. We would get the children down for story time and then bed, our heads would hit the pillow with exhaustion only to be jarred awake to this shrill freakish cry. Sleep-deprived and our faith tested, we plowed forward, sure and certain that change would come.

Our house was an open, rotating door of caring medical and service personnel attempting everything possible to jump-start brain activity in a way that would progress her stifled set of motor skills. Our doors also rotated with people of faith and prayer. Church leaders, small group leaders, and missionaries from around the world descended upon our home. There was great expectation.

Prayer and fasting were commonplace for Molly by us and others. I remember locking myself in a rented cabin at a place called Refreshing Mountain Campground for four days of prayer and fasting. While there, I overheard a man praying in the cabin next door. It was a local pastor. Our prayer journeys were quite different; his journey was about to shift from pastoral ministry to a worldwide church planting endeavor called DOVE International. It would bring forth a great harvest in China and beyond in the years to come. Ours was laying the foundations for a different type of harvest yet to come. Both journeys, although different in so many ways, I believe were equally valued and important to the heart of God.

Kathy's saving grace from slipping into the three-d banks of despondency, discouragement, and depression, seemed to be found in sharing her life and her struggles with others. Her gift of friendship seemed to reciprocate many times over. Thus, when it was her turn to need the help and care of others, they were there.

These were friends she could dump her questions and discouragements upon, not once, but over and over again. To me it seemed redundant, unhealthy, and certainly not faith filled. Yet who was I to question her when it seemed to help her in the moment and get her through another day.

For me, strength came from daily listening to Bible teachers and preachers on radio or on cassette tapes as I went to and from work. Even on the jobsite, the radio was cranked to capacity, loud enough to hear over the sounds of our rapid-fire Black & Decker drywall screw guns. Then at bedtime I listened to a special cassette tape player that could play six tapes without having to flip the cassette! I bought the whole Bible on tape and theorized that my spirit never sleeps, so why not feed my spirit the Word of God while my body sleeps? This particular version of the Bible on tape was dramatized: the strong loud voice that read the Word was accompanied by special background music and sound effects. It was not your typical soft go-to-sleep music by any means.

Quite memorable was the second or third night into my new hair-brained idea. I was sleeping peacefully but Kathy got jarred awake by the loud voice telling the story about Jesus walking on water. With the story was the background sounds of high-pitched howling from the winds and waves on the Sea of Galilee. I could barely "see the gal" the next morning due to a black eye caused by her leap across me and the bed to yank the power cord out of the wall so she could get some of her own calm restored! The cassette set was deemed straight from the pit, never to be used again, according to my now sleep-deprived wife.

Heavily impacted by the teaching of what some termed the word of faith movement, I was learning to speak only words of hope and life and I declared most every day that "Molly, you have a great hope and a great future! You are above and not beneath. You are the head and not the tail. You are favored of the Lord."

Eventually our two approaches balanced out, and we reached theological normalcy. Somehow, by God's grace, it worked, and in my heart of hearts I believe our Heavenly Father was smiling right past our doing the split on the doctrinal dance floor.

This I was beginning to learn: God does not mind our questions, and there is an open invitation to dine, dialogue, and commune with Him. What sane earthly father would not take delight in his son or daughter asking tough questions? I was beginning to see that our Heavenly Father is no different.

During those early years, I was not the best listener for Kathy. Her retelling the same story grew tiresome. But she claimed that sharing her pain had value. Each time she told the story it was like peeling another layer off an onion. As each layer was peeled, she got closer to the core. Her core belief was that God could and would heal her emotions and trauma. I am forever grateful for those ladies in her life who listened, who prayed, and who sat with her. It was a common sight, their talking and sharing life around the kitchen table. Few had answers but they were like angels in the moment, sent from heaven with a listening ear. Nary a one was cut from the same cloth as Job's three friends.

On that hill far away, the shape and size of the old wooden cross Jesus hung upon is an iconic emblem made up of one vertical beam and one horizontal beam. My bifocals seem to measure out a tad more length in the vertical-sized beam, but neither beam is more important than the other. The horizontal beam which carried Jesus's out-stretched arms always represented to me a picture of God reaching out and using others to draw us to Himself. Kathy seemed to lean toward a horizontal approach to finding Christ and often found answers from Christ through others. I tended to be a bit more private, more vertical. I just went straight to God. We were learning to hear God's voice each in our own way.

Molly was helping us define how to relate to God.

CHAPTER 5

FIVE LOAVES OF PROVISION

Shrill screams jarred us from deep sleep and barred us from a full night's rest for most of Molly's second year of life. But this was all about to change. From the very beginning of our marriage, when we discussed our desired family size, Kathy and I always agreed on five children. It just was. It was a knowing that somehow five was God's plan for us.

Around the time Molly was sixteen months old, I reminded Kathy of our vision. My recollection is the discussion was somewhat one-sided. She didn't think five was such a good idea anymore. I, on the other hand, was sure God would heal Molly soon, and I persisted that it would be lack of faith to give up on our desire for five children. Kathy would say she was not giving up on the dream, just the timing of it. Somehow I won out, and we soon found out Kathy was expecting our fifth.

Lest one begin to believe I was an uncaring, unsympathetic husband who had no empathy for my wife who was already caring for four children, with one who needed a lot of extra care... I did actually have a real sense that having a fifth child sooner rather than later was a good choice. If we waited too long we probably would have talked ourselves out of it.

To bring another child into this world would send a strong message: don't operate out of circumstances; don't give up on your desires based on momentary circumstances; don't delay your dreams until everything is in perfect order. I also felt it could be quite healing to Kathy and to Molly's older siblings.

Sharing our good news with others was another story. I just tried to smile and make the best of it when I told them we were expecting our fifth child. This despite having to deal with jaw-dropping, blank-eyed stare insinuations from Kathy's friends,

"What were you thinking?!"

"You did what?!"

It would turn out to be a great call (just put me in the "Hall of Great Premonition"). Matthew Robert Hess was born on January 24, 1996. He arrived so fast the doctor and nurse had to catch him before he hit the floor.

Matthew was some kind of joy indescribable, unspeakable, and almost unbelievable. His sisters now had a live baby doll of a little brother who responded on cue with a coo. His older brother Joseph, now nine, and until then the lone son, was undone. He could not wipe the smile off his face for days to come. He had a brother! Somehow we felt complete. We felt joy again. We felt blessed to see some normalcy again. Each little action, each little movement, each little smile brought renewed strength and life to us all. A newborn brings great joy to any home, but for us, because of Molly, the joy this little boy gave us was multiplied like Jesus' story with the boy that brought to him the five loaves and two fishes. We felt full. We felt satisfied. We were overjoyed by God's provision.

From the exact day Matthew came home from the hospital, his sister Molly stopped the shrill cries in the night. No explanation, no gradualness, no warning; she just stopped. She slept all night, every night, never to wake us again with those shrill, blood-curdling moments.

Emily was the forever doting little mommy. She seemed to float on air between keeping up with her older siblings and the very hands-on care with Molly and little brother Matthew. It was not uncommon for her to carry them around on her hip. Molly was no easy child to carry. Emily was a born nurturer and caregiver. She always seemed to know what to do and who needed what in the moment. As Molly graduated from stroller to wheelchair, the two would crank up the music and twirl on the makeshift kitchen dance floor.

Joseph placed a ball in his brother's hands before he could hold a bottle. Caution was thrown to the wind regarding playing ball in the house. Molly took the brunt of a few errant throws.

Kalah would practice and play on the old upright piano. Molly was always wheeled right there beside her, listening and making sounds to the music, as she seemed to have a keen memory of repeated songs. Music became a saving grace to Molly, as walking, talking, and eating were still not a part of her life's journey.

Molly was defining real joy, real togetherness.

Kathy and Molly (age 5)

Molly (age 5) and Dad

Matthew, Joseph, Molly (age 4), Kalah, Emily

"Blessings"
By Laura Story

We pray for blessings, we pray for peace
Comfort for family, protection while we sleep
We pray for healing, for prosperity
We pray for Your mighty hand to ease our suffering
And all the while, You hear each spoken need
Yet love us way too much to give us lesser things

'Cause what if Your blessings come through rain drops
What if Your healing comes through tears
What if a thousand sleepless nights are what it takes to
know You're near
What if trials of this life are Your mercies in disguise

We pray for wisdom, Your voice to hear
We cry in anger when we cannot feel You near
We doubt your goodness, we doubt your love
As if every promise from Your word is not enough
And all the while, You hear each desperate plea
And long that we'd have faith to believe

When friends betray us
When darkness seems to win
We know that pain reminds this heart
That this is not, this is not our home
What if my greatest disappointments or the aching of this life
Is the revealing of a greater thirst this world can't satisfy
What if trials of this life
The rain, the storms, the hardest nights
Are Your mercies in disguise

CHAPTER 6

LIFE IN THE FAST LANE

A sudden jolt of fear jarred me back into reality as I eased our van off the interstate, onto the exit ramp, and coasted up to the traffic light. There in front of me was a medical delivery van. My lack of planning came racing to the forefront of my thoughts as I suddenly remembered I had given permission for medical supplies to be delivered to our house; more specifically, I said that if we were not there, the back door would be unlocked, and I gave the company instructions for the delivery person to walk in and leave the items on the kitchen table.

However, our morning church plans had changed because Molly, dealing with a cold, was home alone! That's right, home alone. Our son Joe had gone to church Saturday night and graciously offered to hang out with Molly while we went to the Sunday morning service. But he gave us repeated verbal notice that very morning that he had to leave promptly at one.

The van clock said it was five after one in the afternoon, and we were just pulling up to the exit...still about five minutes from home. Just ten minutes earlier, we assured Joe that he need not worry, that we would be home shortly, so he could go ahead and leave. Like grandfather, like grandson, "Unslow Joe" was out the door at exactly one o'clock.

The image of a delivery van potentially arriving before us, discovering Molly alone and not knowing her brother had left only minutes before, produced visions of my mug shot posted on front pages of local and national newspapers. My normal relaxed smile was gone, and I tightened my grip on our conversion van's steering wheel.

Being so close to home, I knew the automotive lay of the land quite well, well enough to know that as you turn left at exit traffic light number one, you have two lane options to go through traffic light number two. If one has the need for speed, when the first light turns green, it is very important to quickly ease into the less congested right merge-only lane.

Once in the right lane, the key is timing. The moment light two turns green, the need for speed is preeminent.

All this I did, and to get an even better edge, I watched the pedestrian signal, waiting for it to turn yellow. I needed that extra split-second jump on the delivery van.

In the left lane, positioned firmly in first place was the medical van. In the right merge-only lane, I was in pole position. The light changed to green, and I left my Sunday morning sermon on preferring thy brothers in the dust. But WHOA NELLIE! The van driver, not to be outdone by some family guy in a van, had similar NASCAR-type thoughts!

But my home-field advantage gave me a slight edge. It was just enough to nose our van in front as the lanes merged to one and thereby forcing the delivery driver to slow his pace to avoid hitting my rear bumper as I careened into the lead.

I was pumped, and by now the family was whoopin' it up with me. Well...not the whole family. Kathy gave me one of those Norman Rockwell-type, freeze-framed, raised-eyebrow looks. She was thinking ahead as she does so well. Her furrowed brow, fully comprehending the moment, had a scow. I read her mind. This now seething, heavy-breathing medical van driver who I just cut off was most likely the same guy who would be showing up at our house in about three minutes!

My visions of expanding my driving career into the Daytona 500 got flushed as I rushed to re-configure my next steps. I decided my saving grace could lie in accelerating through the final traffic light, light number three, now just a quarter mile ahead, and hope the med van got stuck with a red.

This could give me the needed precious few twenty extra seconds or so to arrive at our house and park the van in the driveway. The "unslow" anointing had to flow. I would make an all-out full-speed sprint into the house. I would plop down and act like I had been there all along. I would pull up a chair next to Molly, breathe slowly, and hope against hope that the van driver did not recognize our van—the one with smoking tires parked in the driveway.

The plan was working like perfection. Well, except my planned vision was slowly losing acceleration with my family. My rocking them from side to side, screeching around corners on two wheels, and my lapse in clearly conveying my vision of racing into the house before the van was hardly turned off... Well, let's say my plan was an epic fail of biblical proportions. Oh, I made it in. My dear wife and children, however, got to meet the guy in the driveway as they walked into the house...carrying their bibles. I sheepishly watched out the kitchen window.

My wife, rarely speechless or without words, was speechless and had no words.

It would be occasions like this, after the fact, that had us laughing 'til the cows came home. Laughter proved to be a huge help and healing to us. Laughter was therapeutic; it was real, and I could hardly get enough.

We took Molly everywhere we could. Molly seemed to take a liking to funny stories. She was smiling more often, not always on cue, but heart-warming when you got a smile out of her. Our friends and families accepted her, loved her, and always made space for her.

We had a campfire area on our property on a spot secluded by trees and overlooking the Conestoga River. Conversation and song often continued until one or two in the morning. The kids would fall asleep while the grown-ups solved the world's problems. Late one summer evening, the bonfire got a little too big and got out of hand, and fire trucks showed up to quench the fire. In his report, the fire chief mentioned a disgruntled man in a yellow shirt. Yes, this was our overprotective friend. To protect the guilty, let's just call him Carl. Campfire Carl would not be quenched. We had many more late-night conversations around the fire after that.

Having time away from the kids was not a priority initially, but friends sought to make it happen. For Kathy's thirty-second birthday, our small group sent Kathy away for a weekend to Willow Valley Resort accompanied by a scrapbook of encouraging messages. Matthew went along, as he was just two months old. Her friends must have forgiven me because I was allowed to go too.

We eventually got excited about a twenty-two-hour road trip for a Shultz reunion in Minnesota, thanks to a rented RV. The space afforded Molly the comfort of being able to lay flat for periods of the long journey. From Minnesota we headed straight south to Kansas to visit my sister Sue and family before circling back home to Pennsylvania.

For our fifteenth wedding anniversary, our family and friends encouraged us to get away for some time alone. This was the first time the two of us had extended time together without the children. We tapped a newly married couple, Matt and Kelly Mylin, to watch our children, who at the time ranged in age from three to twelve. They came and stayed at our house for the entire eight days we were away. They passed the caregiver test with flying colors. I'm sure the experience was great preparation for ministry, as twenty years later they would take on the role of lead pastor role at The Worship Center.

When our children were a bit older, we embarked on another RV trip through the Rocky Mountains in Colorado then up through Wyoming. This two-week trip was made possible by the much-appreciated help of Kathy's parents who stayed with Molly for one of the weeks in Glenwood Springs, Colorado and then Molly joined us for the second week.

Kathy's sister Karen helped organize friends, family, and church in raising funds for a handicapped van. Up until that point, we had to lift Molly out of her wheelchair and into an over-sized car seat then put the wheelchair in back. The funds they raised were combined with matching funds from the well-known Joni & Friends ministry which helped to make it all possible.

I found a slightly used high-top conversion van for sale that came equipped with a rear electric lift for Molly, and it came with six captain chairs. Of course, Molly's siblings were ecstatic about having their own swivel seats, and the icing on the cake was an installed TV and VHS player, which was quite uncommon in that era. My friend Billy could tell a story like no other, and he embellished the van to be known as the largest family van this side of the Mississippi…and everyone knew when the Hesses arrived!

People were simply drawn to Molly. She was an attention magnet, even though she never spoke a word. She had a smile that would change your day. It was a smile that told us a real person resided inside her semi-contorted body. It told us, once we looked beyond what she could not do in the natural, that she had hidden normalcy.

The Smucker family went to the extent of breaking-and-entering our home, if you can call leaving your house unlocked breaking-and-entering. They took the liberty of taking some of our old home videos when they knew we were not home. They took the lifted goods back to their house and used their very own home-editing equipment to compile an amazing video put to music titled "Molly Smiles." I like to think this videography gave their younger son, Carson, a start to his eventual career. He currently heads up a staff of eight employees who produce all the Carolina Panthers' football team's preseason promo, game-day, and postgame highlights videos.

One summer at our church's annual outdoor tent service, Kelly Daniels, a missionary from and to Central America, was leading a healing crusade. Some of Kathy's friends picked up Molly out of her wheelchair, each grabbing an arm or leg, and they carried Molly forward and up onto the stage. It was like watching in real time the story of the four friends with the paralytic that cut a hole in the roof and lowered him down to Jesus.

Faith on behalf of someone else is a precious gift. These are things not easily forgotten, not by us, Molly's family, and certainly heaven has record of all the calls, cards, notes, books, and meals. People believed with us. People believed in us. Expectation surrounded us.

Molly was helping us define joy.

Emily, Kalah, Don, Molly (age 12), Kathy, Matthew, Joseph

"Sovereign Over Us"
by Michael W. Smith

There is strength within the sorrow
There is beauty in our tears
And You meet us in our mourning
With a love that casts out fear
You are working in our waiting
You're sanctifying us
When beyond our understanding
You're teaching us to trust

Your plans are still to prosper
You have not forgotten us
You're with us in the fire and the flood
You're faithful forever
Perfect in love
You are sovereign over us

You are wisdom unimagined
Who could understand Your ways
Reigning high above the Heavens
Reaching down in endless grace
You're the lifter of the lowly
Compassionate and kind
You surround and You uphold me
And Your promises are my delight

Even what the enemy means for evil
You turn it for our good
You turn it for our good and for Your glory
Even in the valley, You are faithful
You're working for our good
You're working for our good and for Your glory

You're faithful forever
Perfect in love
You are sovereign over us

CHAPTER 7

THE WORLD'S A STAGE

It was the Friday night before Matthew's first ever basketball game. Now in fourth grade, he was allowed to be a part of "Little Lions," and, oh, was he ever excited. He had thus far lived in the shadows of Joe, Kalah, and Emily who played basketball for Living Word Academy, and under Coaches Burns and Casey they all had quite successful teams in the CCAC league.

Matt lived for these games as he loved going to watch his older siblings play. He and his cousin Zach and the coach's son Nate would paint their faces white and purple, the school's colors, and race through the crowd trying to whip them into a frenzy of enthusiasm during winter basketball seasons. For a small Christian school, the team drew quite a crowd. So tight and intense was the fan base that local lore had it that some passionate, but not-so-referee compassionate trio of dads (Workman, Frey, and Vanderzell) were banned from sitting together in the same bleacher section. The fear was they would feed off each other's fanatical referee-slaying frenzy.

So Matt's turn was coming. From fan to future phenom was his dream. As I tucked him into bed that Friday night, sleeping in the jersey to be worn the next morning, he asked me, "Dad, do you think the stands will be packed tomorrow?"

I had to tell him the truth, which was that probably only a few parents would be there to watch on a Saturday winter morning. But this I promised him, that if he worked hard, was a good teammate, and would use his talents for the Lord, that someday his time would come.

His stage came eight years later as a senior playing his final high school basketball game for the Lancaster Mennonite Blazers. It was the PIAA State Quarter-Finals. There was an overcapacity crowd of nearly three thousand screaming fans cheering on their teams at a neutral playoff site at a school in Hershey, Pennsylvania. Matt was an unselfish player and averaged slightly more than ten points per game for the season. But this night the team went cold, and they desperately needed him to play a role larger than defense and ball handling. He poured it on. There on his largest stage ever at that point in his basketball career, Matt scored a career high twenty-nine points.

The coach of the college of his choice was at the game scouting some other players, but he reached out to Matt a few days later and asked him to join their team. Matt got to use his talent in college.

And, yes, Molly came, and Molly watched, and Molly's sphere of influence expanded yet again. She impacted the players and fans of Messiah College. Just her presence somehow God would take and use.

Matt would one day write...

> *Emotion wells up inside of me every time I talk about you, Molly. Since somewhere around my high school years and the time I started college, I haven't been able to say your name in a context that is deeper than surface level without starting to cry. Even thinking about your life when I'm by myself automatically brings tears to my eyes.*

Godfrey Zawatski, the retired-by-day, photographer-by-night for Messiah College's basketball teams would write...

> *We became attached to her the very first time seeing her at a Messiah game. She was such a beautiful young lady. We remember her smile. We are grateful to have known Molly, albeit for a short time but a wonderful time.*

We all, like children, value being watched, being encouraged, and as Shakespeare once said, "all the world's a stage." Molly's future stage would be a little less defined. We searched for significance.

From the get-go, the various service agencies applied Herculean-type effort. They cared. They sought change. They valued their work. They valued Molly. Karen, the occupational therapist, worked tirelessly. Krystal, a gal from church, was an amazing extraordinary caregiver to Molly in the early years and was one who prayed with and for Molly often.

Our Amish neighbor Abner did a lot of contracting work in the neighborhood, and he graciously allowed his daughter Mary to come once a week to help with chores and with Molly. Our niece Katrina came to help us and lived with us during her senior year of high school.

There were so many… There was a constant effort put forth by the IU-13 program at Reidenbaugh Elementary, and then at Conestoga Valley during Molly's middle and high school years.

All worked with great attention to detail and care for Molly. They all searched diligently during those early years for ways to get Molly to communicate. They tried eye movement, hand movement, even an electric wheelchair was granted in hopes to spur on discovery of decisive, precise, or intentional movement.

But nothing of great neurological significance came for Molly…until around the age of ten.

As she was driving home after dropping Molly off at her specialized school one day, Kathy heard the music of Nicole C. Mullen playing on the radio. It was her song titled "Redeemer." The lyrics and music moved her. She immediately re-routed to the local Christian bookstore to buy the recording for Molly.

That night, after Molly was tucked in bed, the CD was put in and the music began and Kathy left to scurry about getting other things done around the house. But sounds came from Molly's room, sounds loud enough to cause us both to wonder if everything was okay. Upon checking on her, all was okay, but her expression was pained; it was clear that sound wanted to well up within her. And it did. It was not a soft effortless sound, but rather a sound she had to work at. It was not melodic nor did it sound on tune. Yet as we listened to both her and the music it was clear that she was trying to worship along with the song.

The next night we played it again, and again she put forth great effort. These were definitely new sounds and new efforts. Something was welling up, something was being released from within her spirit. Something was different. When "Redeemer" ended and another song came on, there was less effort and less emotion, or even no emotion or reaction to the other songs. It was as if she understood the "Redeemer" message. It was as if there was a spirit connection, like a deep, deep desire to proclaim with whatever she could muster that yes, her Redeemer lives!

Nicole C. Mullen would describe the song this way:

> *"Redeemer" was inspired by the scripture passage in (the Old Testament Book of) Job of when, while under his afflictions, Job stooped and said, "I know that my redeemer lives and at the last day, He will stand upon the Earth." And how he was going to see God with his eyes and in his flesh—not another but He himself. How powerful that regardless of what we go through, regardless of what the world tells us, that we can stand up with our shoulders back and our head straight and forward and say, "I know that I know that my Redeemer lives in spite of what I'm going through, in spite of what I've seen or what's going on around me."[1]*

---

1 Songfacts.com, 11/19/2019, https://www.songfacts.com/facts/nicole-c-mullen/redeemer.

Night after night we played the CD. Night after night "Redeemer" produced the same reaction. It became her heart song.[2]

In an ever-so-small way, we began to understand the importance of heart songs. The now famous story of a man imprisoned for seventeen years in a Soviet jail cell for simply sharing Bible stories to children is shared worldwide in the book, Insanity of God by Nik Ripken, which begs us all to find our own unique heart song.

Around May of 2006 I came across a billboard advertising Nicole C. Mullen, by now a Grammy nominee and DOVE Award winner for the "Redeemer" song. She was the featured artist for a three-day tent crusade located about an hour away from our home. The hope was that her music would bring the unsaved to the evangelistic meetings led by the ministry of Steve Wingfield. I decided on short notice to take Molly. We arrived rather early and quickly noticed the sawdust-laden floor inside the tent, as it was not the easiest to push Molly through. The Virginia-based evangelist made his way right over to us and introduced himself. I tried to be humorous and said something to the effect, "Well, actually, Sir, Molly didn't come to hear your preaching. She came to hear Nicole C. Mullen."

He smiled and took it in stride, thanked us for coming, and then generously offered for us to come backstage to meet the singer after the service. True to his word, after the singing and preaching that night, he came down front to meet us and led us to the makeshift backstage tent. We spent about ten minutes together as I in-

2 Nik Ripkin, Insanity of God (Nashville: B&H Publishing, 2013).

troduced Molly to Nicole and told her a little bit of Molly's story, and then with rather unusual forwardness, I asked if I could pray for her. I remember telling her I was going to pray specifically for her new song "When I Call on Jesus" and prayed that miracles would flow out of her ministering that song. I'm not sure how she felt about that at the time, but it was what I felt to pray.

If one's ears were turned heavenward that night, one would have heard the sound of hammers and nails. Construction was starting. Molly's stage was being built. A small and seemingly insignificant event was defining both her and her family's future.

Molly was defining the significance and power of personal worship.

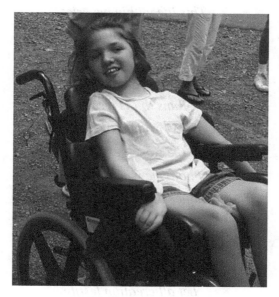

Molly (age 12)

"Redeemer"
By Nicole C. Mullen

Who taught the sun
Where to stand in the morning
And who told the ocean
You can only come this far
And who showed the moon
Where to hide till evening
Whose words alone can
Catch a falling star

Well I know my Redeemer lives
I know my Redeemer lives
All of creation testifies
This life within me cries
I know my Redeemer lives
The very same God
That spins things in orbit
Runs to the weary
The worn and the weak
And the same gentle hands
That hold me when I'm broken
They conquer death to bring me victory

Now I know my Redeemer lives
I know my Redeemer lives
Let all creation testify
Let this life within me cry

I know my Redeemer

He lives to take away my shame
And He lives forever I'll proclaim
That the payment for my sin
Was the precious life He gave
But now He's alive and there's an empty grave

And I know my Redeemer, He lives
I know my Redeemer lives
Let all creation testify
Let this life within me cry
I know my Redeemer lives

CHAPTER 8

WHIMPERED CALLS ON JERICHO'S WALLS

Scoliosis became a serious issue the summer of 2006, and the doctors said we needed to find an orthopedic doctor and schedule a spinal fusion without delay. As we received this news, a dream I had when Molly was around three years old came to mind. In the dream, I was searching the phone book for a name, something like a Baltimore Association of Orthopedics. At the time, I had no idea what the dream was all about or why I would dream such a thing. Neither did I know what an orthopedic doctor did. But I always remembered it.

Fast forward ten years, and, of course, I began looking for orthopedic surgeons in Baltimore. It led us to a team at the Johns Hopkins University Hospital in Baltimore, Maryland. I would not regret this decision. Without muscle tone due to never being able to walk, Molly's spine had begun to slip into an "S" shape. It is a typical pattern and problem for cerebral palsy patients, and despite my faith declarations, Molly fell into this category hook, line, and sinker. She needed a rod infused into her spine.

Surgeons told us they like to wait as long as possible to have the surgery because once the rod goes into the back and it is fused into the spine, patients do not grow any taller. From the time we met the surgeon to the time we scheduled surgery in mid-November it was four months. In that short time span, Molly's spine really took a severe and literal curve for the worse. By the time the surgery date came, her lungs and heart were severely compromised.

We were told that Molly's surgery would not be easy, not by any stretch of the imagination, and that there was great risk.

Joseph was in his second year of Temple University studies in Philadelphia, Pennsylvania. Kalah was a senior transfer to Lancaster Mennonite and Emily too was there as a sophomore. The girls for the past four years had played year-round sports. Both played fall field hockey at Mennonite but with the move to the bigger school they both chose to sit out the winter basketball season. This would be significant as we were heading to Baltimore, so they would be home after school to manage the house and watch over Matthew, who was now in fifth grade. Kathy's parents, Harold and Alma, were to be a huge help to the home front as well.

Kathy and I headed to Baltimore with Molly for what we thought would be one to two weeks. We hoped to be home for Thanksgiving. Molly was whisked into the operating room to get prepped. We kissed her goodbye, said a blessing and prayer over her, and headed to the waiting room. It was a long wait.

About four hours later, the doctor came rushing in to inform us that Molly flatlined. Only 70 percent of the spinal fusion was done. Her heart stopped beating, and chaos ensued. They had to quickly flip her on her back, still not stitched back together, of course, but they were able to resuscitate her. Then, as they tried to flip her over to finish stitching together her open back, she flatlined a second time. Yet again, they were able to regain her breathing. But with her back still cut open, and the rod not completely tied in place, the surgeons were in a very difficult place. It was decided that the fusion could not be completed until Molly regained some strength.

To make matters worse, Molly was at great risk of spinal injury if she had any sudden movements, even something as minor as slightly moving her head to one side as she commonly did. They ordered her to be in a locked down, fixed position with no movement at all. Her head was placed into what I can only best describe as a Christmas-tree holder turned upside down. There were screw-type holders protruding from the "halo" that had to be tightened against her skull to prevent her head from moving even a fraction. It was unbearable to look at.

And so it was. Our Thanksgiving was held in Baltimore, and by mid-December, the surgeons assessed she had perhaps regained just enough strength and stamina for them to try to finish the task. Molly really was worn down both emotionally and physically, but they could wait no longer. We were told it would be touch-and-go, life-or-death, and if she came through, recovery might be weeks, possibly months.

They completed another six hours of surgery. She was heavily sedated, and then we waited. Christmas was spent in Baltimore. Family brought us meals, friends brought us cards, calls, and flowers... There was a steady, almost daily, flow of friends and family coming from Lancaster, Pennsylvania to spend time with us at the Johns Hopkins Hospital in Baltimore, Maryland. We celebrated the best we could. Either Kathy or I was with Molly while the other one was at home with the household. Kalah, Emily, and Matt held down the home front quite well. Somehow Kathy felt I should still try to coach Matt's Saturday morning basketball team. It was certainly a healthy reprieve.

It was New Year's Eve day, our twenty-third wedding anniversary, and late afternoon when we were suddenly summoned by the doctors as we returned from our walk around the hospital block. Molly flatlined a third time. I remember calling my sister Rachel and brother-in-law Bruce to ask for prayer because I was too weak to pray at that moment. I was ready to let Molly go.

Kathy and I, with our weak arms lifted heavenward, mustered enough courage to say, "Molly, it's okay. You have fought well. We release you to go to heaven if that's what you want. We will not hold you back any longer." It was one of my lowest moments.

Molly was resuscitated once again, and ever so slowly, she began to recover. She began to pull through. Little by little, she gained strength. She seemed to have an inner will to fight for life. Her time on this earth was not finished. The surgeons at Johns Hopkins saved her life. The prayers of the saints saved her life. There was more for Molly to accomplish. Faith and trust persisted.

That same week, late one evening as I was pacing and praying, the story of the Israelites marching around the walls of Jericho came to mind. Putting faith in action, I got in the car and drove around the city blocks of John Hopkins Medical Center seven times. It was midnight, and I am not sure if the security cameras had my car pegged for strange behavior or not. It mattered little. This I was sure of: Mourning would be for the night. Joy would come... Surely joy would come one of these mornings.

Molly's aunt Krista had a memorable encounter while staying with Molly at the hospital. Krista and her husband, Dan, were such a big help in so many practical, non-assuming ways many, many times over the years. In this instance, she had traveled the ninety-minute drive south to Baltimore to give us a reprieve to go eat or sleep. A visitor to the bedridden child next to Molly had been there for a few hours, and Krista noticed her packing up and leaving for the day. But about ten or so minutes later, the visitor came back and asked a question.

"Are you this child's mother?"

Krista explained she was Molly's aunt. The lady then said, "As I was leaving the hospital, I just felt compelled by the Lord to turn around and come back and tell you this: the Lord says this child is going to be healed!"

By early January there was talk of moving Molly closer to home, which would mean transporting her by helicopter to Hershey Medical Center (HMC) for further recovery and a possible tracheotomy. I will never forget helping unload Molly off the helicopter following her forty-five-minute flight from Baltimore to Hershey. Molly came off the helicopter looking about as wild-eyed as I had ever seen her, and if her eyes could have spoken, they would have said, "Wow, what a ride!"

The kindness, calmness, closeness to home, and just a new change of scenery was healing to all of us. Molly spent another four weeks at HMC under the watchful eye of Dr. Mikula. Molly brought with her very deep bed sores due in part to the difficult and longevity of stilled bed rest and recovery from Baltimore. Her lungs also were slow to recover.

There was to be a tracheotomy, agreed upon and scheduled in Baltimore, but tasked for the Hershey specialists to carry out. The evening before the appointed surgery, Dr. Mikula said, "Give her one more night's rest, and see how she is in the morning."

In the morning, the tracheotomy was canceled. We were forever grateful. By early February, almost four months later, Molly returned home.

That was a happy day.

These were trying times. These were times of little understanding as we watched Molly suffer. Perhaps because of the dual reality that the song "Redeemer" comes from Job, and that the book of Job is about suffering, I was often drawn to these fascinating discourses. God's longevity of grace was evident in allowing five men to speak their minds, thoughts, and ideologies. His gospel is a long-suffering gospel. I was beginning to see that God is never hasty in His answers. He allows us to churn and turn, all for a purpose of hope and desire for us to discern His will and to discover who He really is. Even if it takes a lifetime, it seems to matter not.

Yes, there comes a point where He eventually steps in to correct and rebuke the sin of spewing out the wisdom of mere man, which was the case of Job's three friends. But they were forgiven by God when Job prayed for them, and Job's misfortunes became double blessings after he repented for speaking words that were not truthful about his Creator. Job was doubly restored.

Eli who? Elihu is a character I became infatuated with. His bursting on the scene around chapter 32 came with a fullness of the spirit, wisdom beyond his youthful exuberance, and though vehemently disagreeing with his elders that spoke before him, he was honorable to them in his actions. He seemed bent on the call to repent; for one to take personal action for correcting fallacies regarding the character and nature of God. His words gave evidence of a God that so loved his people that He would allow them to go through pain, yet only for the intent of saving one's soul. Intriguing was the fact that Elihu was not named as one of Job's three friends forever recorded as being rebuked by God.

The doctrine of the sifted saints is not an easy task to unmask. In her book *Visions from Heaven: Visitations to My Father's Chamber*[1] author Wendy Alec attempts to sort this out with a rather unordinary, contradictory script unreflective of her Rhema University diploma. The word of faith movement affected many, myself included, and I would say in a very positive way. Highlighting

---

1 Alec, Wendy. Visions from Heaven: Visitations to My Father's Chamber, (Dublin: Warboys Publishing, 2013).

what I would term vertical Christianity, the word of faith folks emphasized believing the Word is what it says it is, a belief that the gifts of the Holy Spirit are for today, and that just as all should be saved, all should be healed. Much to the dismay of the university founder, I would read articles about some of their graduates muddying the message with an overemphasis on the doctrine that God wants us all to prosper monetarily.

Ironically, the weaknesses of the movement, in my opinion, would be a fear that just one wrong confession could take away the "hedge of protection" mentioned in Job 1:10 (AMP). I have known some to take it to the extent of never mentioning to others that they or a family member were actually sick or dying... until they died. There was a fear (ironically) that Satan could gain leverage if we dared verbally to release an ill-spoken word.

The teachings I heard on Job were explained in such a way that it was fear that opened the door to let Satan gain entrance into one's life. This was based on Job's own words, "For the thing that I greatly fear comes upon me, And that which I am afraid has come upon me." (Job 3:25 AMP).

Wendy Alec's take on the matter is interesting and is one that I am doctrinally willing to commit to more study. The author would clarify her point that these words of fear were Job's words, not God's words about Job. She would say that God saw Job as righteous. It is Satan that sifts the saints, and God is there to aid and pull us through these times of sifting.

In Job's case, there was a lot of loss. I cannot imagine losing all one's children, as Job did. But I was beginning to see that God views loss differently than we do. Death here is life elsewhere. Life much better elsewhere. Those who are victorious in seeing God as righteous, those who do not blame God, those who forgive others and correct their own misrepresentations of who God is, these are in line for God's restoration.

Kathy was becoming a magnet for those trying to deal with life's hardships. Molly was a visible representative for many to identify with. She lived her life as an open book and would find His presence and His peace through weakness. She would term herself as desperate. It took humility to share her pain with others. Kathy had no issue with speaking what she was going through. Hers was a belief that when Humpty Dumpty fell off the wall, all the king's horses and all the kings men could put all the pieces back together. In her own so-called fall from the wall, it was the queens of discourse that came calling. These were ladies who would listen lots, share a little, and who would pray together. She built her faith around trusting God working in and through others for a way out. She placed great value in sharing her pain and being healed through walking out her faith in the presence of other believers.

I liked what I saw and did not touch it. Relating it to fatherhood is about the best way I can explain it. As a father, there is no greater joy than to see your children grow in interacting with others. To watch them live to bless others brings deep-seated joy. Provision does not have to come directly through the Father!

As mentioned before, this I would term as horizontal Christianity, and quite honestly, it is something I believe both the church and the world are desperately craving. Conducive to a healthy church is deepened relationships shared around caring for one another. The world struggles with believing in a Spirit being and horizontal Christianity delivers heaven to earth via God's own children sharing with others.

God loves to see His children bless one another. There is no competition in whether healing and restoration comes directly from Him or through His children. It's all the same.

Molly was defining His healing presence coming through others.

CHAPTER 9

THE GOLDEN BIRTHDAY

It was now early November of 2011, and I awoke with the thought, *What am I going to do for Molly's eighteenth birthday?*

Molly would turn eighteen on December 18, which we referred to in our family as one's golden birthday...December 18 matched the age Molly was turning. With little time to ponder the first thought, the second thought about rolled me out of bed, *Invite singer Nicole C. Mullen to Molly's golden birthday!*

The thought was so out of character that I couldn't shake it. More out of embarrassment than anything else, I did not tell anyone for a few days, though I sheepishly searched around on the internet to see if I could find out any more info. Sure enough, it was easy to find. A few more days went by until I got the nerve to send an email asking if Nicole would be in our area around the weekend of December 18. I secretly hoped I could feed off some other group that had already booked her in our area. I feared to ask the cost because I was having a rough year in business and had no extra cash flow to make something like this happen. Nor did I have a clue as to what it cost to bring a singer of her national caliber from Nashville, Tennessee to Lancaster, Pennsylvania.

Sure enough, Karen, her booking and concert manager, saw my email and called me. I sheepishly gave some very sketchy details about what I was after. I am sure she thought I was some sort of emotionally washed-up dad trying to gain sympathy for his daughter. My stream of consciousness was going a little haywire in trying to explain that Molly really likes Nicole's music even though she had never told us she likes it. No, she doesn't talk, but somehow she makes some sounds, so we are sure she likes it. By now I was getting in deep and could not find my way back. The manager was gracious, however, and she gave me some options on costs for bringing a smaller version and not the whole band.

The cost was still way beyond what I had. I actually had no available cash at the time. By this time we had left our prior church to help with a church plant in Elizabethtown (chapter 11 will cover these details). The idea came to call our former church, The Worship Center, to see if they would work with us to share the cost to bring her in… As God would have it, the church had wanted to invite her to sing for several years!

I shared this idea at our midweek fellowship group, and they too got excited about a Christmas concert with Nicole and Molly. Funds came together from family, friends, and our new church, LifeGate, for our portion in a matter of about a week! The Worship Center agreed to their portion, and it was set. Nicole would sing during their Saturday night and two Sunday morning services, and we would have her sing at Elizabethtown College's Leffler Chapel on Sunday evening December 18.

The Sunday night birthday celebration was billed as a Celebration of the Father's Heart: A Night of Worship with Nicole C. Mullen. Many came together to give time and money. Ruth Martin from LifeGate church put forth great time and effort into making some awesome posters to advertise the concert. Her daughter Sonya, one of our church worship leaders, even wrote a special song for the event. With all the upfront giving, it was now deemed and advertised as a free event with a freewill offering that would go to local ministries.

Over five hundred people showed up for Molly's birthday party. WOW! What a touch of heaven. Molly's nurse Sarah loved her part, which was getting Molly all dolled up and looking like a celebrity. The local newspaper heard about the event and showed up. My oh my, what a special eighteenth birthday party it was. God's blessing was upon it; heaven felt close and seemed to rain down blessings upon us all. Nicole of course sang, "Redeemer." People still talk about it to this day. It was a night to be remembered, a night when family, friends, and community gathered together to bring value to a little girl named Molly, a little girl who never spoke a word, yet she worshipped in her own little way, each and every day. Her heart song was heard from heaven. Her personal worship was elevated out of the bedroom and was now joined by hundreds of others in a beautiful night of worship.

Her impact upon us was growing. Understanding was coming about worship, about how it leads and prepares the way for heaven to invade earth. Day and night, night and day, like incense, Molly's own version of worship was reaching heaven. In turn, it was opening up heaven for us. God responds to the cries of worship. He hears. He cares. He moves. The event evoked a well-written summary and reflections by one of LifeGate's pastors, E. Daniel Martin. Here is an excerpt:

We prayed that first of all the Lord's name would be lifted up, that His love would be celebrated. We prayed that the evening would be about Him and not any of us. We prayed that Nicole C. Mullen, in spite of her great fame, would minister in a spirit of humility that lifted up the name of Jesus and not her own gifting. We prayed that even mistakes would turn out to the glory of God and that there would be a strong sense of the presence of God in the meeting. And yes we prayed that Molly would be healed; that she would speak a word indicating that she does understand the love of the father and the mother and the brothers and the sisters.

And God did answer prayers. There was a strong sense of the glorious presence of the Lord in the meeting. People were encouraged, inspired, lifted up with new faith and love. Molly did not rise up and walk or talk, but somehow there was a peace about being in the presence of God with her and knowing that God loves her and will not withhold any good gift from her or from us.

We were content knowing that in His own time He will make all things clear, and no good thing will be withheld from Molly or us. And in the time before all things are clear or mended, we continue in faith and hope and love.

Our hearts were stirred as Sonya Penya sang "Molly's Song," the song she had composed about Molly. As she sang this song over Molly, as Molly sat in her wheelchair next to the piano, a tear was noticed in Molly's eye. And as the tear slowly trickled down Molly's cheek, Sonya's voice broke as she sang, for she thought, "Molly does understand; she is moved by what is happening tonight."

Molly was defining what God's favor looked like.

Molly and sisters Kalah and Emily pose for the camera

Nicole C. Mullen and Molly at Molly's 18th birthday concert

"Molly's Song"
By Sonya Penya

You were sitting on the edge of the crowd
Feeling cold and a little left out;
The Father's eyes scanned the room
And gently fell upon you;
He drew you out of the many
And said, "I have a special plan for you, Molly."
Molly, did you know
That your weakness lets His power be shown?
And, Molly, did you know

That your worship makes your heart His throne?
And did you know that in all these years
He's never left you alone?
Did you know...?
His love, like a fire burns to make you whole
His arms, they enfold you through the questions of your soul
Molly, did you know,
That your destiny was planned before your birth?
And, Molly, did you know there're no words
To express your great worth?
And did you know that in Christ's kingdom
The last become first?
Did you know?

Now on this your 18th birthday
Surrounded by friends and family

Can you hear your heavenly Father say?
Molly, did you know that I sing, I sing—
Molly, I sing over you

CHAPTER 10

MORE FOR SURE

The colloquialism "Living High on the Hog" assumedly comes from farmers living well after receiving top dollar for their herd of swine. My slogan for our 2011 Christmas season was "Living High on the Heavens," as the Christmas and New Year season could not have been scripted any better. December being the month of Molly's birth meant Decembers were particularly hard for Kathy. Memories would come flooding back. A pain filled re-stirring of emotions always seemed to take place right after Thanksgiving, and it was hard for Kathy to really fully enjoy Christmas, as the disappointment of another year with little change in Molly's physical status was made evident.

But the eighteenth birthday concert was a game changer. It was our own version of a Hallmark-type movie that could have been titled "Molly's December to Remember." We would not look at Decembers ever again quite the same.

We were humbled and simply amazed at what God did for Molly, for our family, and the boost it gave our fledgling new church plant in Elizabethtown.

And if that was not enough, the icing on the cake arrived on the front page of the Monday morning Lancaster Intelligencer Journal. There she was; Molly's story made the front page of the paper! Words can hardly describe the joy of seeing a picture of Molly on stage with Sonya singing over her. I still get choked up.

God was also showing us that He has resources available that go far beyond my ability or inability. Ideas come. Ideas need tested. They need shared. Faith comes. Momentum comes then provision typically follows. If one never risks, one will never know the outcome.

I stepped out of the shower just a week or so after the concert, and I heard these all but audible words from heaven, "There will be more."

More of what I did not know, but my immediate thought was it may be related to more music, more worship, or possibly even more concerts. I would ponder that phrase every so often, but in reality, life has a way of racing by. Along came high school and college graduations, weddings, and the best part, eventually the grandchildren. In the summer of 2015, I was involved in helping at our Kingdom Life Network (KLN) conference. KLN is an affiliation of our church plant, and every other year the network members from around the region and world come together for a three-day conference.

Across the table from me over the lunch hour was P.C. Alex-

ander, founder of a great work and leader of two hundred plus
ministers working together into the unreached in northern India. I
had been there twice to see the work. In the midst of our conversation, an opening came for me to ask him if he would consider our
bringing Molly to India along with the Nicole C. Mullen team for
a night of worship for the churches in the capital city of New Delhi. "How would India respond to a little girl like Molly wheeled
onto a stage?" I asked. "Could the churches of the region come
together for a night of just worship?"

The seed was planted, or perhaps we were watering a prior seed.
My first trip to India was in 2010, and P.C. took us to various ministry outposts, schools, and churches. Eventually we ended back
at their headquarters.

Not to dishonor or minimize the value of the evangelists and pastors and schools that are putting feet to an effective work, but what
I came away with as most impactful was the small band of women
that gathered daily to pray. Every weekday, Monday through Friday, they pray for four to five hours per day for the ministry. I was
so impressed by this and so moved at the value that PTL-India
places on prayer that I emailed them a picture of Molly upon my
returning to the US. I asked them to pray for Molly.

There is no doubt our planning a trip to India was in no small
part due to these ladies praying for Molly.

Preliminary planning began for the fall of 2016, but it became
quite clear that this was not going to be an easy task. For start-
ers, the cost was going to be monumental. A tad daunting was

the thought of the cost to fly Molly in her wheelchair, Lisha her nurse, Kathy, myself, and the Nicole C. Mullen team and band. Not to be forgotten was food, ground transportation, lodging, and the concert hall venue rental in one of the most populated capitals of the world.

But keep in mind, these were my thoughts, not His thoughts.

Molly was defining ever-increasing faith.

"Call on Jesus"
By Nicole C. Mullen

I'm so very ordinary
Nothing special on my own
I have never walked on water
I have never calmed a storm
Sometimes I'm hiding away
From the madness around me
Like a child who's afraid of the dark

But when I call on Jesus
All things are possible
I can mount on wings like eagles and soar
When I call on Jesus
Mountains are gonna fall
'Cause He'll move heaven
And earth to come rescue me when I call
Weary brother, broken daughter

Widowed, widowed lover
You're not alone
If you're tired and
Scared of the madness around you
If you can't find the strength to carry on

Call Him in the mornin'
In the afternoon time
Late in the evenin'
He'll be there
When your heart is broken
And you feel discouraged
You can just remember that He said
He'll be there

When I call on Jesus
All things are possible
I can mount on wings like eagles and soar
When I call on Jesus
Mountains are gonna fall
'Cause He'll move heaven
And earth to come rescue me when I call

CHAPTER 11

THE STOREHOUSE

An unauthored humorous story from my childhood is told of two farm boys who climbed a ladder with paint cans and brushes in tow to paint a barn roof. The wind blew the ladder down and despite their hollering no one heard them. Hakey-Jake spotted a manure pile hidden behind the far corner of the roof and convinced his friend Leroy it would be safe to jump off the roof and into the soft landing. He jumped and hollered back up to Leroy to do the same, claiming it was only ankle deep. Leroy finally got the courage to jump, but when he landed he was stuck in manure up to his chin!

Furious at his so-called friend, he shouted, "You said it was only ankle deep!"

To which Hakey-Jake retorted, "That's because I dove in head first!"

There have been times that I have likened owning my own business to that of jumping off a roof. Sudden winds shift the ladder of success, and there are few options but to leap into the steep stuff.

Leading up to this 2016 concert event, an amazing series of events regarding sifting, shifting, and finances needs to be shared. To do the story justice, we have to go back eighteen years prior to 1998. It was early that year (Molly was just four going on five) when I got this strong urge to figure out how to recycle drywall waste. I had been a drywall contractor for nearly fourteen years, and the last four of those years a partner in a company that kept about fifteen to twenty workers busy installing and finishing drywall primarily in residential new homes being built.

An unusual and inordinate amount of thought and passion came upon me. It got to the point that I could not resist thinking and dreaming about how to accomplish something that, to my knowledge, had not been done yet. Each house we installed drywall in had about a ton of leftover scraps from the windows and doors cutouts.

My youngest brother, Dan, was in-between mission assignments and working for me, and I remember discussing recycling drywall on the jobsite. When an article came out in the newspaper about a garbage collector that came up with a machine that would strip the paper off the drywall backing one piece at a time, I felt an urgency to dive in. I knew one piece at a time would not work too well and was compelled to figure out how high volumes could be done.

With a farm background, somewhere in my studies, I remembered that gypsum had soil value. I often surmised that had I went to college I probably would have talked myself out of the venture I was ready to embark upon as it did not make much economic sense on paper. My good friend and partner in the drywall business was Darl Yoder, and he graciously bought out my portion of the business. The plan was for me to exit gradually over a six-month period from that business and commit full-time, by April 1, 1999, to this new venture. The funds from the sale would be used to start one of the country's first drywall recycling businesses.

When an idea comes from heaven, my rationale of thinking at the time was that surely there would not be problems. But by 2003, I was not actually stung by chin-high dung but rather was covered head-to-toe in a rather large pile of unsold drywall dust. Larger still was our debt.

Molly and her issues never really brought me to my knees like it did Kathy, but dealing with financial lack—something I had not encountered until that point—brought me crashing down. The funds from the sale of the drywall business in 1999 were long gone. The trial and error that came with numerous equipment-related attempts to successfully grind, screen, and separate the paper from the gypsum came at a high financial cost.

Eventually we were able to process the material at a rate of twenty-five tons per hour, but not at a profit. I was two hundred fifty thousand dollars in debt, our house was mortgaged to the hilt, and four years later, the business was still not turning a profit. Banks would not help us, and it was humbling to ask for financial help from my dad, brother, and others. I struggled with having to ask friends for prayer and counsel. It was a slow death to self-sufficiency. I literally could not fix it on my own.

Each morning I would wake up feeling suffocated. It felt like a pillow was over my face. I could hardly breathe. A missionary who held an annual conference near Baltimore, Maryland, invited us to one of their meetings. We went, and at the end of the service I went forward for prayer. As hands were laid on me I began to feel like I was going to choke. I could not catch my breath.

And then…it was gone.

"It" is referring to what I now believe was a spirit that was sent by the enemy camp to snuff the life out of me. Spiritual warfare, I was discovering, was quite real.

Kathy often walked and prayed with a neighbor-friend Rhonda Lapp. She and her husband Gid had blessed us in many ways during this difficult financial season; even to the point of lending us a large amount of money from their line of credit until some of our refinancing went through.

It was Rhonda who took the initiative to get us a prayer team specifically to pray for our business. Up until this new business venture, I was quite private about money. I loved to give, as we often had extra, but I was not accustomed to being in this place of lack.

A prayer team was formed, and we began meeting and praying. Within six months or so, change began to slowly happen. A dad of a basketball player I helped coach came to my aid. Robert Hayward was in between jobs, and he took me around to meet various businessmen. A wise and seasoned Christian businessman came to our rescue by agreeing to consolidate our debts in exchange for minority ownership. This put us on much firmer footing, and soon after other things began to shift and move. Some very large orders came our way for both incoming and outgoing product.

With the advent of our prayer team meeting almost every week, and our prayers starting to be answered, we felt inclined to ask the others what we could pray with them about. What were their visions? To this question, some prayer-team members shared their interest in planting a church in the Elizabethtown area. We said we would join.

It was not easy to leave our comfortable blue chairs at The Worship Center, which we had become accustomed to. After all, we had attended for twenty-one years. We raised our family there, were involved in the school, and had lots of friends. To top it off, Pastor Sam Smucker was an awesome teacher of the word of God. The church had grown from about five hundred to twenty-five hundred in those years, and it just really felt like home to us.

So many friends had helped us with Molly. Kathy and I struggled with the change as we felt loyal to our past while we felt the Lord was bringing change into our future. It was a rather hard season. We both had sensed an unrest for quite some time but were so rooted in the trenches of school and church that we were never even willing to ask God what to do about it. We did not want change. We presumed The Worship Center was our home forever.

Agitation, I have found, is a sure sign that change is coming or something has to change. I found myself being more prone to gossip, less gracious to others' shortcomings, and more apt to question leadership. The lesson seen now, but certainly not then, is that if I had actually used spiritual Q-tips for their intended purpose, perhaps I might have heard the Lord more clearly, and the transition might have been less relationally challenging. Our church blessed us in our leaving. We sure had to adjust from the mega-sized church mind-set when starting from scratch.

Our lack of business and personal finances that I define now as our "dying to self-sufficiency," would actually lead us through new doors, to new people, a new school, new church, and a new ministry. Three of our children ended up meeting their spouses from these new church and school settings, which greatly lessened the inevitable pain change brought. I do realize this is putting God in a small box, but I often wonder how He would have brought them together had we not been open to change? The new doors were not necessarily better than the old; it just seemed that we were being shifted for new purposes.

The one area that had not shifted yet was where we lived. The thirty-minute travel one-way to Elizabethtown for church services and meetings two to three times per week had my wife thinking for the first time maybe we should move closer to church and work. Outwardly I smiled but inwardly I dug in my heels. Changing churches was hard enough, and leaving our quaint, red tin-roofed house and nearly three acres that bordered the river was not going to happen…not if I had anything to say in the matter. But Kathy's prayers were heard despite my inner stubbornness.

She was praying for a place halfway between Lancaster and Elizabethtown.

The weeks and months passed; she would start boxing things in the basement and attic from time to time, and I would smile. She would show me properties, and I would smile some more. One Sunday morning we saw an auction sign along the major highway on our way to church, and I commented a tad smugly, "Oh, that's a nice house and barn."

And then I muttered loud enough for Kathy to hear, "If God sells our other farm, I'll go to this auction."

Our other farm was a hundred-plus acres of land but with buildings that were in need of great repair. We had bought it only because seller financing made it possible about seven years prior, and in the process rented out every square inch to keep up with the mortgage payment with little left for the list of needed repairs. I had gutted out the chicken houses, so we could use the seventeen thousand square feet for inside drywall storage.

But as only God could orchestrate, that very week I got a phone call from a realtor inquiring if I would ever consider selling this farm!

"No. It is not for sale," were my very first words.

But the realtor was quite persistent, and said I should at least consider an offer because he had a client who was very interested in this specific area. Unbeknownst to me, land values had risen greatly in the recent years, and sure enough, they were offering a very good price. I decided to listen.

My commitment to go to this newly found farm auction was fresh on my mind, and in the midst of the process, I figured we had better at least take a look at the house and barn. The look took about five minutes. Kathy did not mince words.

"This place to too big! What would we do with a nine bedroom farmhouse? And what would we do with the forty-seven acre horse farm with fences everywhere?"

My entrepreneurial brain saw potential. Yes, we were becoming empty nesters, but Molly needed her own quarters. Matthew was still back and forth between home and college, and what about in-law quarters for one or both sets of our parents?

The auction was scheduled for early Saturday afternoon at one and happened to be during our annual church men's retreat. I didn't give out too much detail to my comrades but asked to be excused for the afternoon and drove the two hours back home to the auction. My son Joseph met me there. The auction moved along rather quickly. It was obvious there was not too much interest by others in this horse farm based on the size of the bidding crowd. Knowing what I was getting from the other farm, and meeting prior with our banker, I knew my limit on the price they would allow me to go to.

I honestly had little confidence we would become the owners, but I would say I had a little smile on the inside, as it seemed like God was up to something. The farm was worth more, in both my opinion and the seller's opinion, than our bid was able to go, but the bidding stopped promptly when our last bid was given. The auctioneer did his best to coax and conjure up more interest, but that was it. The auction stopped. The owners were asked if they were willing to sell, and they were not. So we all went home or, as in my case, back to the men's retreat at the mountain cabin.

But shortly thereafter, I got a follow-up call from the auctioneer who said the owners changed their minds and agreed to sell the farm at our final bid price.

We settled both the sale of our property and the purchase of the new property six weeks later but then rented the purchased house back to the sellers for an undetermined amount of time. Kathy and I were a bit shell-shocked at all this and felt a little like, "What just happened here?"

Six months after the auction, on an early April morning, I said, "Okay, dear, let's do this."

And so we did. In May of 2015, we moved.

Molly would get to move into a large house with her own private quarters with plenty of space for both Kathy and her nurse Lisha who cared for Molly about twelve hours a week. The hallways were wide and spacious for wheelchair mobility, and an area was even designated for a future elevator install.

It just felt like a special gift from heaven for Molly, and one that we too would get to enjoy. And it came with a swimming pool. I had always promised Molly a swimming pool. Eventually Monica "the wonderful," our endearing caseworker with United

Disability Services, would help us install a state-funded elevator. Molly eventually got a second-floor bedroom right next to ours, after having to sleep on first floor make-shift bedrooms most of her life.

My brother Dan had died in a farming accident and joined the ranks of heaven June 2, 2014, just sixteen months before we bought the house, and I still ponder and wonder at times if it was he who tugged on Jesus's cloak to ask for this blessing on our behalf. The whole move just seemed surreal.

But the bigger picture was not so much about the buying and selling of the farms. But rather it was about some funds left over which, as my wife can attest, is quite a rarity in my entrepreneurial career.

We sought the Lord for wisdom on what to do with the excess funds. The option of paying down a portion of our home and business loans was considered and acted upon, but at the end of the day, we desired to give back a portion of what we were blessed with. The story of the woman with the alabaster jar in Luke chapter 7 really spoke to me. To some, pouring out her expensive perfume on the feet of Jesus was a financial waste. But to Jesus it was an act of worship…using something of great value for eternal value. Two thousand years later we still are talking and singing about the woman with the alabaster jar. What she did was not a waste. It had great kingdom value.

The endeavor to create a night of worship in India became our own version of the alabaster jar. Directing our giving to make this happen felt like an act of worship. It felt purposeful, like we were pouring expensive perfume on the beautiful saints of India. Whereas the golden birthday event in 2011 was made possible by others footing the bill, the 2016 event was ours to pay. It was ours to provide. Not an ounce of my business savvy could have pulled off the sale and purchase of these properties in such a timely way, and I very well knew that. I was extremely grateful, humbled at what God did, and wanted to honor Him back in such a way that was unusual and impactful. It was our alabaster jar.

This I am forever mindful that we were granted this precious gift in Molly. Few get to experience the grace one receives from unreciprocated care.

As our good friend Bill Crider would one day say at her memorial service, "There was an aroma of glory around the face of Molly."

And we had the privilege to be in her presence every day. And it moved us.

Molly was defining our alabaster jar.

CHAPTER 12

LET INCENSE ARISE

With funds in hand, planning for the India trip continued. Thankfully we found out ahead of time that we could not take a wheelchair on the airplane. We were thrown for a temporary loop when we realized Molly would have to be carried onto the plane and placed in a seat next to Kathy and her nurse. This little detail complicated our plans because I had planned to leave with a team a week earlier to show them the ministry in India and to help setup for the concert, which meant I would not be with Molly to carry her onto the plane for the Dulles to Frankfurt then Frankfurt to New Delhi legs of the flight.

To better visualize, Molly could not simply be carried upright in front of the person carrying her. She had to be lifted flat and carried horizontally in one's arms. As an adult, she was petite, just eighty-five pounds, but it was awkward weight, and she was somewhat stiff to lift. Kathy and her nurse could lift her from the wheelchair to the bed, but that was an effort. The airplane was another matter. Her contortions and the rod in her back made everything more than Kathy and crew could manage.

And with high-backed seats on an airplane, it would take Herculean effort to carry Molly horizontally and above the seats, which are about shoulder-height high, from the entrance of the plane's ramp to the middle or back of the plane. We did not book first-class tickets in an effort to save on ticket costs; in hindsight, first-class seats would have been helpful. Our strong-armed son Joe changed his plans and work schedule and came to the rescue. He was an eleventh-hour addition and proved to be a game saver.

Kathy's sister, Krista, also a nurse, decided at the last minute to go. She was a huge blessing. For the first leg of the flight, the six hours to Frankfurt went well as there were empty seats for Molly to stretch out on.

Changing her diaper was another story. The tiny airplane bathrooms were out of the question. It took the whole entourage of ladies to hold up blankets for privacy and to change her right on the row of seats.

Each flight meant wheeling Molly to the airplane entrance and then carefully lifting her out so the chair could be stored underneath. Then Joseph carried her horizontally high above the seats until he reached her assigned seat. All this was done both getting on each flight and then off again, a total of eight times, if you are counting. Surely heaven was recording. The second leg from Frankfurt to New Delhi was more of a challenge. There were no empty seats on the flight, and Molly had to sit upright snuggled tightly between Kathy and Lisha for the whole six hours. Upon arrival to the airport, our India delegation met them with great rejoicing that all arrived safe and sound.

The rented wheelchair van with a ramp was eventful. The company's version of safety straps was, I think, Velcro®. I decided not to look too closely. I was just grateful to be there and was so thankful to our ministry partners and friends for showing us hospitality. P.C. Alexander, his son Ashish, and son-in-law Blessan were tremendous hosts and highly organized.

Bonny Andrews, founder of LiveJam, a national youth ministry, was asked by P.C. Alexander to help run the promotion and concert. His team, who had large event experience, was absolutely amazing. Bonny even had a friend who took a four-hour flight from southern India into the northern city of New Delhi just to run the light show.

The concert venue was to be the iconic Siri Fort Auditorium, home to many large musical and political events including the recent hosting of former USA President Obama who gave a speech on the very platform of our event! Tickets were free but directed to Christians in the region, and many came that could not have otherwise afforded such an event. Around fifteen hundred people came to what was billed as ADORATION, a Night of Worship with Nicole C. Mullen. It was an amazing and memorable evening of worship and of lifting up the name of Jesus in the capital of the country, bringing together the churches from various faiths and denominations.

Bonny Andrews opened in worship along with another local artist. P.C. Alexander followed and spoke briefly; then he invited all the pastors in attendance to come forward. Arm in arm they linked themselves from one end of the stage to the other, joining in prophetic prayers and proclamations for their region and for their nation. P.C. would say later, "We are convinced that the fruits of these prayers and proclamations made in faith will be seen in the days and years to come."

A video telling the story of Molly and her love for music and her connection to the song "Redeemer" followed. Included in the video were her sisters and mother sharing the impact Molly had on their lives.

Prophetically pertinent to the moment were these words by her sister Emily,

> *I once had a dream about Molly. In it, Molly was on a stage in front of thousands of people, and I was peeking around the curtain with the biggest smile because I finally got the chance to be on the sidelines cheering her on like she had done for us all through our sports careers and other accomplishments.*

And so it was Molly's time. It was her moment. It was her time. I wheeled her across the large stage. Seated to Molly's right and in the front row was Kathy, her brother Joseph, her Aunt Krista, and nurse Lisha. Seated next to them was my dream team; Chinedum Uwaga, Joe Spence, and Skip McElhenny, the friends who flew over early with me to visit the ministries and help set-up for the concert. Front and center were the Alexanders and with them many of the PTL-India family and staff, including the ladies' prayer team that stirred my heart a few years earlier.

The fifteen hundred patrons present stood. They clapped. They cheered. They teared. They honored Molly. They honored her for her coming, for her worship, and for being the reason for this gathering.

Standing by her side and holding her hand in mine, I spoke these words,

> Tonight our daughter Molly is placed before you on this stage. This is no ordinary stage. This is a stage that has held some of the most powerful leaders in the world. United States President Barack Obama spoke on this stage not too long ago.
>
> The powerful seek and speak of peace. But this little girl named Molly has known and shown peace without ever giving a spoken word. She has shown us that she has value. She has shown us that her sounds of worship reach heaven. She has shown us that worship is from the heart. She has shown us that worship stirs the heart of God and that God in return stirs the hearts of mankind. Heaven and earth move at the sounds of worship. Action is released in the heavens. Shifting takes place on the earth.
>
> I expect shifts to take place in this region, in this nation.
>
> Tonight, Molly takes part in blessing you with a night of worship. My wife Kathy, my son Joseph, our children back home Kalah, Emily, and Matthew, our team that has traveled with us nearly eight thousand miles, extended family and

friends, the small group of prayer ladies in Ghaziabad, the Alexander family, the E. Daniel and Ruth Martin family, our church called LifeGate, our network of churches, the teams from LiveJam and Nicole C. Mullen ...they all are a part of this. We have come to bless you. We come to join in with you for a special, special night of worship. We believe that as you worship, it connects you with the God of Heaven, the One who sent us Jesus, the One who sends us the Holy Spirit ...that tonight He will in turn, speak to you. He will call you to do unusual greatness, extraordinary works of service, great acts of kindness that go beyond the normal.

There is greatness and value in every person. Do not disdain and throw away the lesser among you. Worship tonight. Worship with all your heart. As He has done for Molly, surely He will ...in due season ...as you worship...move heaven and earth on your behalf! God bless you all. God bless, Molly. God bless the music of Nicole C. Mullen.

And so we worshipped. Oh, did we worship! Children raced and embraced the stage to sing and dance as Nicole led. Voices were raised; the spiritual darkness of the region was pushed back. It was a night to remember in New Delhi.

P.C. Alexander would write me this letter:

It was indeed a very special and memorable evening. It was not the first time that a well-known singer was performing in one of the large venues of Delhi. We have had big names visiting with bigger teams, bigger stadiums, and bigger crowds... but ADORATION was different.

The greatness and uniqueness of ADORATION was the message that echoed through this entire evening and also for days, weeks, and months to come. The message was bigger than the crowd and the event itself. The theme of ADORA-TION was nothing other than the "Father's Love.' The event very clearly displayed to what extent a loving father would go to express his love to his daughter. It was an evening where the message of the loving father heart of God was portrayed before the audience.

It reached the heart. There was a strong message for a so-ciety and culture that looked at women in general as inferior and someone with any kind of disability as a liability and bur-den. Ours is a society that is known to leave infant girls aban-doned or even killed before they saw the light of day. A society where a girl with any disability would never be allowed to meet or mingle with guests, and even families. Don pushing Molly in the wheelchair across our stage spoke volumes. It was a memorable moment as the entire gathering stood up and applauded the celebration of a father's love without any prodding from anyone. They were all responding in unison as they saw before their eyes how special, how precious, and how dear Molly was to the Hess family.

A word must be said about Molly's oldest brother, Joe. His being there spoke volumes. His willingness to travel all these miles to help and to be there with his sister while on stage meant "my sister is very special and dear to me and she has value."

Don, Kathy, Joe, and to the entire team, thank you for bless-

ing Delhi. The message you have communicated continues to challenge many even though it's been a couple of years since you came.

Molly was defining value.

Gathering of pastors from the city of New Delhi praying together on stage

India concert 2016

Molly and Dad on stage India concert 2016

CHAPTER 13

A SUMMER
TO REMEMBER

The next day, basking in the sheer joy of the event and eating together at a local restaurant with Nicole and team and extended family from PTL-India, I asked Nicole if there was a country she hadn't been to yet where she desired to give a concert. To my sheer surprise, she said Japan!

To this day, I am not sure why I asked her that, as it was not on my list of preplanned questions. Actually, I had no list of pre-planned questions. But the mention of Japan instantly sparked a "there will be more" moment inside my heart. My older sister, Sue, is married to a Japanese American, Dr. Yutaka Kawase. They are the parents of five children and have made numerous trips over the years from their Kansas home to Japan to share their gifts of creative worship and dance along with a message of hope and reconciliation through Jesus.

Certainly, Sue and Yutaka carried us in their hearts over the years despite the many miles between us. I remember a specific moment when Sue's heart was touched for Molly. It was the end of a Hess family reunion spent in Massanutten, Virginia. Some of us had traveled to my brother Jim and sister-in-law Rosemary's church after the reunion. At the end of the church service, some of us gathered in the back of the church to say goodbyes. But Sue had a desire and unction to pray for Molly. And when she did, deep wells of intercession came upon her. Her praying came to my remembrance when Japan was mentioned. One can only wonder what deep intercession eventually produces.

The Japan trip idea was briefly mentioned to the Kawases upon our return to the US, but it was placed on my inactive shelf with the hope it would come together down the road.

About a year and half later, now the spring of 2018, Molly's health took a unique turn. It was hard to put a finger on what was different; it just felt different. Her ability to change from a cold to a warm season was always a challenge, but her cold and congestion lasted longer than usual.

My honorary roles of unpaid Head Respiratory Doc and Chief Pulmonologist became increasingly needed. The latter role involved getting Molly to cough up phlegm and time the suction tube insertion with precision. The two of us were quite good at working together at it. It was certainly not a glorious job in any way, but somehow, I had the grace for it.

Her coughing could be rather intrusive to the common bystander, as it was typically constant, and rarely did she have a strong cough. Her inability to swallow made suctioning a normal, necessary, and important part of maintaining her quality of living. In addition, her breathing would grow labored and shallow, which required oxygen support. Molly's spells would typically last two to three days in a row or a week at the longest. This spring, however, it was unending.

It was unsettling, and I confess I was a tad irritable. Kathy can attest. Molly's congestion seemed unshakeable week after week. Some prolonged swelling in the ankles noticed by her nurse Lisha was out of character. Doctor visits seemed not to turn up anything out of the ordinary. She made it through her younger brother Matthew's wedding in June, thankfully, without too much issue. Our desire to get away for an extended weekend in early July was in question, but her nurse encouraged us to go and graciously held down the fort.

Coming into the summer of 2018, I was getting a little antsy about the "Japan thing" and asked the Lord for three specific things regarding Japan: first, that there still would be a spark of interest from my Kansas sister and family in pursuing and being a part of a Japan worship event; secondly, that Bonny Andrews would be able to connect with Sue and Yutaka and family as both he and they would be an integral part of any future Japan event; and lastly, it was on my heart to somehow connect the Kawase family with Nicole C. Mullen, as much detail and dialogue would have to go into planning to be on stage together for such an event.

About three weeks before our family reunion, I was enjoying some fresh air while mowing grass with our fun Ferris zero-turn mower and noticed a WhatsApp message that came through to my iPhone…all the way from India. It was the 2016 concert event coordinator, Bonny Andrews, and after turning off the mower, a little chitchat took place back and forth texting on the phone. It did not take long for him to get right to the point. He asked if I knew of a place to stay on short notice in America for about four-to-five weeks. That was a tad bold of a text I thought, thinking perhaps he was asking us for housing. We had a family reunion coming up that would fill up our farmhouse bedrooms, and we had other guests arriving before and after the reunion, so I kindly responded by text (if that is even possible) and mentioned that our place would be full.

But I did remember the Penyas; they are this amazing God-filled family from our church. It was Sonya (the wife) who wrote the amazing song for Molly's eighteenth birthday concert and Horeb (her husband) who videotaped the event. The Penyas received the needed money just that week to take their entire family to South America for the summer to minister into the Venezuelan refugee crisis. Their house was now empty, and as it turned out, just what the Andrews family was looking for.

God had forespoken to Bonny about spending some time away from ministry and told him it would be in America. This by no means was a habit for them just to up and leave India. But that very morning they were informed by their contractor, who was working on their house in New Delhi, that they had to vacate the premises immediately because mold was discovered during re-pairs. Bonny seized the moment. His dear wife did not.

Kalpana informed him she would only go to America if the finances came in and if they had a place of their own. She was holding out for her heart's desire for some true family time. She was not envisioning shared living in a hotel or with another family.

The finances came, and wow, this house and property in Elizabethtown was an answered prayer to the T. It even had a state-of-the-art treehouse in the backyard with an attached zip-line for their two young boys to enjoy.

Within twenty-four hours the Andrews had their cupboards, furniture, and belongings completely boxed and put in storage, so the house could be repaired, and their suitcases packed for America. I picked them up at the airport thirty-six hours later in Philadelphia at three in the morning. By five they were in Elizabethtown. They arrived just ten days prior to the start of our annual Hess family reunion where nearly eighty family members, local and from around the country, would gather at our farm, and yes, the Kawases would be there.

The first person to arrive at our house for the July 19 through 22, 2018, family reunion was Yutaka. Barely beyond the normal greetings were these words, "So let's talk about Japan."

Things were stirring. That was Thursday morning. And on Friday night, Bonny Andrews was at our house and briefly met the Kawase family.

Meanwhile Molly was still struggling. We kept her upstairs in her bedroom away from family. On Saturday morning, as Kathy was changing her and getting her up and out of bed and into the wheelchair, she actually thought perhaps Molly turned the corner, and she could bring her downstairs to join the reunion. But suddenly what ensued was what she could best describe as some type of seizure. She summoned for me, and by the time I got there the seizure-like activity had just ended, and she collapsed in a deep quiet.

Yutaka and their oldest daughter, Jenna, now also a doctor, raced to her room. A brief evaluation followed, and then the need for an ambulance was determined. Molly was whisked away to Lancaster General Hospital.

We had been through the hospital routine frequently since her bout with spinal fusion some ten years prior. Often it would take a week or two of antibiotics to help her get over the prolonged cough that would make her ever so weak. But this seemed different. The swelling increased.

Back at the reunion, the Kawases were flying back to Kansas via the Baltimore-Washington International airport (BWI) on Sunday afternoon. Sometime during the reunion, the unction to check Nicole C. Mullen's concert schedule came up. Lo and behold, of all the places in the country she could possibly be on a Sunday afternoon, she was performing at a large church near BWI!

"Who does concerts on a Sunday afternoon?" I wondered.

The thought crossed my mind to check in with her manager to see about arranging a short Kawase visit, perhaps after the concert. But between the family reunion at our farm and my being by Molly's bedside at the hospital, nothing got done until around four in the afternoon on Sunday afternoon. Sue texted me that their plane was delayed while they were on the way to the airport, and that they might actually be able to swing by the concert venue to meet this singer if I could arrange it.

My cell phone battery was on 2 percent and stayed there for ten minutes as my text went through to Karen, Nicole's road manager. She had to get clearance from the home church, making sure they would not be dishonored with an outside group barging into their event. The Kawase clan numbered twelve with spouses and grandchildren. The hosts graciously allowed it. I sent off the address and contact info to Sue...and my battery died.

Four hours later I found a charger for my phone and sure enough, I got a picture of the Kawase family with Nicole C. Mullen and band. They had a glorious fifteen minutes of connection and prayer. A Japan tour seemed imminent to the heart of God.

Our plan, of course, was that Molly fully recover and be a part of it. A week later, on the Sunday night of July 29, I was leaving the hospital around nine thirty and walking out to the parking garage. Molly was settled and in good hands. Friend and prayer partner, David Kandole, remained at her bedside and was praying. Bonny Andrews, Mark Focht and others had been coming and going throughout the day. A call came from Calvin Greiner. Calvin is a great treasure to our region. He is one who walks and talks as if Jesus is right beside him in the flesh. When Calvin talks, I love to listen. As he spoke to me on the phone, he could barely control his emotions and heartfelt words. He kept saying,

"Molly and Jesus. Molly and Jesus, they are so close. He is with her. He is so near her. They are together."

That was Sunday night. Just five days later, on Friday afternoon, is when I awoke to hear Molly talking to Jesus.

"I am going to remember this day as long as I live."

Saturday was chaos. As she was transported from the Intermediate Care Unit to the Intermediate Intensive Care Unit, her breathing tube became disconnected. Pandemonium ensued. No less than ten doctors and specialists pounced on her situation. Literally. Her heart plummeted. They injected needles right into her heart to keep it going. I watched, prayed in the spirit, and gave her once again to the Lord. What seemed to be the last possible second before she breathed her last, they got the tube reconnected. Air entered her lungs and her heart regained rhythm. To hear her heartbeat again was like music across the monitors.

Staff gave some shouts, some huge sighs of relief, others some out-loud verbal prayers of thanks. But honestly, now looking back, I don't think she was even there in her body to feel a thing. Friday seemed to be her day with Jesus.

On Sunday we gathered around her bedside; she looked comfortable for the first time in quite a few weeks as dialysis was starting to drain the excess fluids out of her. We left for home to get some sleep. In the early morning hours of Monday, around three thirty, we got the call to return. Her heart rate was dropping. We were there within twenty minutes, but by the time we arrived, she was gone. The peace of the Lord was upon her face. They had already removed all the tubes. The swelling was gone. She was still warm. We called her siblings together and spent an hour or so together around her bedside. Heaven was with us. Heaven was now her home.

Molly defined perfect peace.

CHAPTER 14

CHAPTERS UNWRITTEN

It seemed Molly was ready for heaven. She had done her work. She had struggled enough. She had lived to see each of her siblings married. She had impacted them in so many ways, far beyond what we as parents could ever do. God spoke to them each in unique and in different ways. Each a journey of their own.

The timing of Molly's death here on this earth seemed perplexing in regard to Japan, yet so right on all other fronts. Different ones would say later they sensed it was her time to go. It was just these unplanned, uncoordinated series of events seemingly pointing us in the direction of moving forward in blessing Japan with worship…but this could go on regardless. It could be done in her memory.

There comes that moment in every believer's life when the cross is not understood. The disciples did not see the cross coming. I did not see Molly's death coming. This is not how I pictured it ending.

This is not how I told my children it would end. This is not how Kathy and I expected it would end.

But the grace and presence of God was with us. It was as if Molly had a deeper understanding than we did. It was her time. It was heaven's time. Her life had touched us deeply. Her work on earth seemed done. Her worship had reached heaven. Her worship had, in turn, touched earth.

The memorial service planning began. Calls, texts, and emails from all over descended upon us like warm refreshing rain.

There was a deep sense that this was going to be a special memorial service. The week was filled with planning, tears, and more planning. A prior graveside private service for Molly at Kraybill Cemetery was planned for Sunday morning, and The Worship Center, having the space and the ability to livestream the service, graciously agreed to host the Sunday afternoon memorial service.

At our children's request, we chose cremation instead of the traditional open casket. This allowed us the unusual opportunity to bury Molly's wheelchair. Her ashes were placed in a box and seated on her chair. Her chair was her home. Her chair was a symbol of her limitations. Her chair was so uniquely shaped that it would not be of much use to any others. Her chair would be buried with the certain hope of her body gaining a new and better resurrection.

On a quick pre-trip checking out the gravesite prior to the service, my son Joe rode along with me to the Kraybill cemetery. We shared a holy moment together as he stammered out, "Dad, all I can say is 'well done.' You and mom loved well. You did well.

Well done."

Those were memorable words from a son. I could only reply with a tear-stained nod.

Sunday came. Our ministry network friends, David and Grace Kandole and Chinedum and Nkechi Uwaga, gave direction, input, and song as we gathered around at the cemetery's shallow-dug grave. These were brothers that prayed consistently with me for many years. David was at our house most every Thursday morning from six thirty to seven thirty along with friend Bryan Hahn. With Chinedum, it was prayer every Tuesday night over the phone. When we were done he would often sing a song over Molly as I held the phone to her ear, and inevitably she would smile. It was an honor to have these brothers direct the graveside service.

Molly's aunt Krista, one that held Molly near and dear to her heart, one who shared closely the many traveled miles with us on this journey, made this poignant statement:

> *The past week the thought was there that this may be the preparation time for Molly's wedding...that her bridegroom is calling her. I had this picture of Molly in a white dress with a ring of flowers in her hair. I didn't have a sense of timing... if this was going to be soon or sometime in the future. So on Monday, I believe Molly took her own walk down the aisle as the bride of Christ!*

Highlighted were these words from Kathy:

> *Molly, you kept alive our desire for the miraculous, and to*

press in to knowing God more fully. You were a gift I didn't always know how to receive, but you were a constant reminder to me of how precious and valuable life is, and to never let go of hope.

Our sons Joseph and Matthew along with our daughters' husbands Seth Lamb and Matthew Weaver together lowered the wheelchair, each holding a corner with an attached rope, into the ground as family and friends gathered in closer...and we worshiped.

Indelibly etched in my memory is our then three-year-old grandson Jake peering down into the hallowed grave. The grave would be forever the recipient of Molly's wheelchair. Her impact was already formative and impactful to Jake, his younger brother, Landon, and cousin, Lucas. They were drawn to Molly. They would push her around the big kitchen as she sat in her wheelchair. Or they would crawl right up onto her chair and sit on her lap.

Jake now watched as Molly's grandfathers each took a turn using the shovel to drop dirt into the hole. Others then joined in. Her nurse Lisha and husband Robert, with tear-stained faces, took a turn with the spade. Aunts, uncles, her siblings and their spouses also joined in this way of saying goodbye to Molly and covering over this wheelchair symbol of her past, not in regret but rather with great joy, knowing it was no longer needed. Molly now had a greater resurrection. No longer was she bound by a wheelchair. She was running, prancing, dancing in the flower-filled fields of heaven. No more pain, no more strain, and with a voice without waver.

"Oh death, where is thy sting" (1 Corinthians 15:55).

She was free...free at last.

We gathered for a noon meal put together by her aunt Linda. She too always held a special place in her heart for Molly. It was Linda who organized a family prayer chart covering us in daily prayer the first year of Molly's life. It was she who arrived just in time to see the ambulance take Molly from her home here on this earth just twenty days prior. Linda seemed always in the vicinity when comfort and care was needed.

Upon our arrival, about an hour early for the two in the afternoon service, the church was a scurry of activity. Our friends Tina Frey and Fan Smucker had gathered others to help organize tables of pictures and mementoes of Molly. Carl Smucker, the now infamous man with the yellow shirt and thief-turned-video creator of the "Molly Smiles" production, had that particular video showing on the lobby screens as well as the video used for the India concert.

It was service time and our son-in-law Seth, surely living off the prayers of many, had the strength and power to lead the worship, and our niece Natalie joined him. It seemed heaven was with us from the onset. Those gathered on this Sunday afternoon of August 12, 2018, totaled well over four hundred, and another three hundred would watch by livestream or eventually watch it on tape delay. Extended family in Kansas, Colorado, North Carolina, Barbados, Ethiopia, friends in India, all were able to tune in. The two-hour service was filled with worship, a video of Molly's life and travels, and sharing from individuals from specific seasons of Molly's life. E. Daniel Martin brought the initial message which then gave way to Luree Yoder and Billy Crider sharing about the early years. My brother Jim represented our families, Don and Doug Lamb represented the Elizabethtown region, and Bonny Andrews sang and shared about the impact of the India concert. And then it was each of Molly's siblings. It was the highlight of the service to hear their journeys with the Lord and Molly.

It was Matthew, whose unrehearsed, un-coerced open letter to Molly during her hospital stay and subsequent allowance of our posting on social media that garnered a lot of Molly-focused prayer and attention. Here is a portion:

I want to know why it couldn't have been me instead. It just doesn't seem right. And it also doesn't sit well that God didn't even give you a voice so that you could complain or speak up about it or defend yourself. When I reflect on my own life, I've made mistakes, and it would at least make sense for me to be punished. But what have you ever done? All you have done is sit there and smile despite it all.

I still trust in God's plan for your life, and my trust in God will never waver. I fully believe in His goodness, and I fully believe he loves you more than I can understand. I know that His thoughts are higher than our thoughts and His ways are greater than our ways. But that doesn't stop the emotion that wells up inside of me every time I talk about you Molly.

Emily would follow with these heartfelt words:

I'd crawl in bed with Molly and tell her about my day and the drama at middle school I was going through. I'd write in my journals about wanting so badly to hear Molly respond back, and I wanted to have that big sister role of giving her advice and caring for her needs. As I got older and was out of the house more often, I'd make a point to spend time with Molly when I was home in the evenings. I'd turn on music and we'd dance together in the kitchen, and I'd play with her hair and rub her feet. I wanted her to know how much I loved her because I would have this guilty feeling that she might get lonely as we all started getting older and moved out of the house. Looking back, I am certain that she was never alone as God always had his angels with her.

Molly's siblings seemed each to have their own individual and personal wrestle with God. Kalah's wrestle came in the midst of an off-campus college worship night when she sensed God asking her, "Will you still declare my goodness, even if your sister is not healed?"

At that moment I realized how much of my faith was tied up in when God heals her...Then I will proclaim His goodness, I believed. How many of us get caught up in the "even ifs"? Will you declare His goodness, even if that one thing that you most want to happen, never happens?

I grieve because I miss Molly, and I am sad that I did not witness her physical healing. Yet God did keep His promise.

113

Molly is healthy and whole, with her Creator in Heaven.

And this portion of Joseph's words at the memorial service:

In many ways, Molly defined our family. I'm ashamed to admit that for many years I fought that definition, believing it to be a negative characterization. Don't get me wrong, I loved Molly and felt deeply for her, but her physical challenges made certain things a lot more difficult for our family. They radically changed the responsibilities thrust on my parents. They made it more difficult to go out to eat or on family vacations. It was sometimes embarrassing to sit in church or go out in public because she would attract attention.

In my mind, the goal was always to minimize the impact she had on our lives—that somehow making sure we had a "normal" life was the best alternative available. It took several years, but by the time she was a teenager, we started to recognize that in many ways—in arguably the most important ways—she defined us as a family. But far from being a bad thing, we realized how blessed we are that she did.

Molly gave our family the ability to rally together. To spend more time with one another. To confront the difficulties of life and to be better prepared for the challenges to our faith. We saw firsthand from our parents how one reacts to suffering. How a mother and father support one another in the tough times. And I'd like to think we siblings were examples to one another. I can't tell you how much joy it brings me remembering so clearly Molly sitting by the piano, smiling while Kalah practiced her lessons...or Emily dancing with her in her wheelchair in the kitchen...or Matthew crawling over her as a baby. She brought so much joy to our home. And it is a privilege to be defined by someone so special.

Some highlighted words from Kathy and I as we closed the service:

We are and have been surrounded by communities of faith, hope, and a future. Kathy and I and our children are here today to say thanks. Molly could not have changed so many lives without your giving us love, care, and kindness. It's been so deep, so rich, so real.

Molly, without ever saying a word, has touched lives around the world.

Nicole C. Mullen wrote us a note this week saying Molly "now knows our Redeemer in ways that we can only dream about!"

I wonder sometimes if Nicole would have ever written the song "Redeemer" had it not been for some hard times? That one song affected Molly, affected our region, and affected India.

We will go and we will do...because of Molly: because she liked her music; because she knew her Redeemer lived; because others need to know.

By the end of the book, Job comes to realize his smallness compared to God's greatness. Who but He can tell the sun where to stand in the morning? It is He who tells the oceans you can only come this far.

Our questioning God as to whether He is good and just in our or others' circumstances puts us on the throne. Then we become the judge as to what we deem fair. And that, we have experienced, is not a place we want to be. Let's not go down the path of disappointment in God. Let's not get so consumed with the how, why, and who did us wrong. Rather let's consume ourselves with how we can respond with words of faith and hope.

In the early morning hours of Monday, August 6, her heart on earth stopped beating. But Molly's heart for her brothers and sisters, her mom and dad, and for each one of you here today forever beats again.

"Everything"
by Lauren Daigle

Even the sparrow has a place to lay its head
So why would I let worry steal my breath
Even the roses, You have clothed in brilliant red
Still I'm the one You love more than this

You give me everything
You give me everything
You give me everything I need

Even the oceans push and pull at Your command
So You can still my heart with Your hand

You tell the seasons when it's time for them to turn
So I will trust You even when it hurts

You give me everything
You give me everything
You give me everything I need
You give me everything
You give me everything
You give me everything I need
When I can't see, You lead me
When I can't hear, You show me
When I can't stand, You carry me
When I'm lost, You will find me
When I'm weak, You are mighty
You are everything I need

You give me everything
You give me everything
You give me everything I need
You give me everything.

CHAPTER 15

YET THEY DO NOT SEE

John the Baptist most assuredly walked in his calling. Born to a mother well past her time and a father unmuted at his son's first cry, he grew up sensing a special purpose for his life. Yet even John has questions from his prison cell.

"Are you the one who is to come, or shall we look for another?" (Matthew 11:3).

Life was not making sense to the cousin and forerunner of Jesus. Shortly thereafter, his head was handed to Herod on a platter.

And then there is the hall of faith chapter from Hebrews 11 which overviews some of the greatest-of-great exploits of yesteryear's heroes. These were men and women of unusual strength, courage, anointing, and valor. Yet mixed right in with the great victories over kings, kingdoms, and Red Sea partings were those who died not seeing their victories...those who died yet still believing!

How can these be honored amongst the great ones?

How can those sawed in two be named in the Hebrews hall? One could brew on that one for a while.

Time and again the Bible honors faith and those who walk in it. Faith is elevated to pinnacled heights when the Hebrews writer wrote, "Without faith, it is impossible to please Him."

God-type results come only through faith. But the Bible is clear that when the results come is for Heaven to decide. Answers to prayer will come. Faith trusts regardless if the answers come today, tomorrow, or next week. Faith trusts even if we die before seeing the end results.

The walk of faith gets a bit messy. Kathy and I would reflect often that life would have been a lot simpler had we just accepted Molly as having issues too difficult to manage. It would have been easier to hire others to make her as comfortable as possible and focus solely on our other four children. But our calling seemed sure. We believed we were called to live out a life of faith in front of others despite seeing limited physical change during Molly's life.

Faith takes that which is and dares to believe for more than what we can see. Faith is like a muscle that needs repetitive workouts to remain strong.

Faith can be offensive as it does not agree with phrases like, "Don't count your chickens before they're hatched."

Faith appears proud, yet in reality, it humbles us. It can take a boatload of courage to speak what the Word of God says about an unseen matter. On the contrary, it takes no effort to speak what one already sees.

When devouring the stories and teachings of the miraculous in my formative years, my filter of thinking and processing began to go the direction that one could rise above any problem by applying faith. My theology did not allow for much grace for people who stayed sick.

Yet trying to live out a life of faith can lead to misunderstanding. Through the eyes of a child, after years of hearing us and others proclaiming that Molly would be healed, our son Joseph would say it felt like we were telling a lie. It caused me to think and ponder more deeply the message of faith and how it relates to our daily living.

Quite often the issue becomes our speaking forth in faith what one "hopes" to see happen. This is based on the reading or hearing of someone's experience. For me personally, I surmised that because Jesus healed the man with palsy, surely he would do the same for Molly, because she too had a type of palsy.

My study of the book of Acts, my reading hundreds of books on past and present moves of the Spirit, they all included the miraculous. So I had no problem knowing healing is God's expectation for each new generation. My understanding was and is that God is an unchangeable God. What He did for one, He surely would do for another. He is the same yesterday, today, and forever according to Hebrews.

Yet the question begs to be asked, "Why are not all healed?"

I am not certain I will receive all my answers this side of glory, but this I do know from scripture, John 10;10 says, "The thief comes to steal and kill and destroy."

If we are followers of Jesus, we are called to war against the attacks of the enemy. We do not simply give in to whatever comes along. Jesus was our example. He came to set people free from sin, sickness, and disease…not put it on them.

We took this to heart for Molly, and most every day we declared His Word over her. It was not religion. It was not duty. It was not trying to convince God. We just felt led to bless her with words of life.

Words like, "Molly, you have value. We see you healed and whole in all areas, spirit, soul, and body. You have a great calling. You are above and not beneath. You are blessed of the Lord. You are a worshiper. God hears your prayers. He is with you day and night, night and day."

For the record, Molly loved this. Most every time she would smile. Her mind and spirit was whole and normal in so many ways, but I have to trust the Lord to give us absolute clarity some-day about why her body was not. I still am quite surprised that her physical body never did respond here on earth.

A pastor friend of ours shared this fascinating account that sheds some character and enlightenment into the nature and ways of God. Granted it is a secondhand story, but he was right there to hear it directly from his brother-in-law right before he died. This brother-in-law had a visitation regarding the judgment seat of heaven just three days before he passed away. He was a deeply religious man and was quite rigid in his doctrinal beliefs according to my pastor friend. In his weakened and about-to-die state, the man expressed some doubts about his salvation and whether his works on earth had merit in heaven.

The man saw himself standing before a very long table. On the man's left was Satan, and on his right was Jesus. At the other end of the long table was the Ancient of Days, and so glorious was His splendor and brightness that he could not see his face. Satan wasted no time in lashing out accusation after accusation as he pointed his finger at the man and screamed, "Guilty! This man is guilty! He did not love his wife unto death!"

On and on the rant continued. The Ancient the Days gave a nod to his left, the man's right, just a slight motion with his head, as if to say, "Step in behind Jesus."

This the man finally understood and slipped in behind Jesus. Immediately Satan was confused and seemed disoriented, and he kept looking around as if he lost the man. Eventually, seeing the many beautiful things to look at, curiosity got the best of the man, and he stepped out from behind Jesus to get a better look. Immediately the accuser attacked him again, this time swinging his long tail, which smacked the accused to the floor. When he got up, he again saw the head motion and nod from the Ancient of Days and, knowing what He meant, he slipped back in behind Jesus. Again he was protected.

A third time curiosity got the best of him, and the man stepped out from behind Jesus. Again the accuser venomously attacked him, this time saying, "This man used your name in vain! He tried to heal others with the Name of Jesus!"

It was true. The man prayed for someone to be healed, and they were not healed. The man realized in that moment that he spoke "In Jesus's name" without ever getting clear instructions from Jesus to do so.

The story and visitation made me ponder. Many times, regarding Molly or otherwise, I too spoke what I hoped to see happen or what I saw Jesus recorded as doing in the four gospels. But as the Gospel of John would correlate with this man's visitation, He wants us to do these things out of a relationship with Him and a trust in learning to hear His voice. He wants to give us His instructions. He wants to speak to us. Romans 8:14 says, "For all who are led by the Spirit of God are sons of God."

Interestingly, each miracle Jesus did was a bit different. There was no cookie-cutter seven-steps-to-healing formula. There was only one formula: do what the Father showed Him in secret in public by faith!

For one man, Jesus spat on clay. For another, He instructed to pick up his mat and go home healed. Still another, He just spoke the word as He was not even present to lay hands on the person. The key seemed to be He did only what the Father showed Him to do. This is quite a learning process, and yes, mistakes in hearing instructions clearly will be made.

I believe the Lord delights in our trying. Think of new parents enjoying a toddler trying their first steps. Falling is part of the process. We learn to grow in hearing, in trusting, and in application. If we err, rather err on the side of trying. God is not harsh. He loves our trying. He loves our exercising faith.

But woe to those who shrink back and never risk. It is pride and fear that keeps believers from trying, from asking, from believing for something beyond themselves.

My journey of understanding faith became more about, yes, believing for the miraculous. But even more-so, in my journey I was going to trust God regardless of whether or not I saw the miracle on this side of heaven. The key was to keep activating faith but to trust a bigger picture that I was not completely privy to. If you read Kalah's full version of sharing at the memorial in the footnotes she, in a quite vivid way, also came to this same revelation, "Will I trust Him even if?"

It is a test every believer needs to pass if they want to be used by Him. Whether it is healing, a lost family member, mentoring a recovering alcoholic...faith cannot be thrown on the trash heap the first time things don't go our way. Keep at it. Keep believing for change. Keep laying hands on the sick and reaching the lost as the Lord leads. Don't let a few bad experiences affect your future faith. It is the evidence of things unseen! You don't get to see it first!

I'm so thankful we surrounded ourselves with a faith community that dared to believe, a community that exercised their faith with us.

I had an experience as an eighteen-year-old while at Youth With A Mission's Discipleship Training School in Salem, Oregon. I read the passage of Thomas doubting Jesus's return from the dead; he had to see it to believe it. He had to see Him first. The grace-filled reply of Jesus to Thomas was burned like a branding iron upon my spirit in that very moment when I read the passage, "Blessed are those who have not seen and yet have believed" (John 20:29).

There was an immediate knowing that this would be a life verse.

From the very beginning of creation, life was not always about fairness. It was not about the good guys always winning. Abel did the right thing and yet got killed! He offered what he knew to be pleasing to the Lord and it cost him.

"Though he died, yet through [this act of] faith he still speaks" (Hebrews 11:4b, AMP).

Molly died, yet she speaks. She offered the most pleasing of sacrifices when she worshipped the Lord each day. She did it the best she could. It was what she chose to do. It was what she could do.

Did she not have faith to rise up out of that wheelchair?

I don't know.

Did we not have enough faith?

I don't know.

Did not the hundreds of others who prayed over her not have enough faith?

Who but God knows the conversations between Jesus and Molly?

Could it be Molly let go of the right to be healed here on earth for a greater and higher purpose to be accomplished in others?

Could it be she endured for a season upon receiving assurance that her plight would cause others to question God? And in that questioning the door would open to dialogue with the Creator of the universe? And what if in that dialogue they would discover Him?

Perhaps she bore this momentary affliction for your and my eternal gain?

Paul inked to the Corinthian church the admonishment of, "Now I know in part; then I shall know fully, even as I have been fully known" (Cor. 13:12b).

I have chosen to leave these answers to the One with far greater understanding. I have chosen to leave it in the hands of the One "who tells the sun where to stand in the morning,

who tells the oceans, they can only come this far..."

He is the Most High.

He is just. He is fair.

Molly helped us define faith.

CHAPTER 16

ARIMATHEA AROMA

Joseph of Arimathea was there at the death of Jesus. He did not understand, but still he was there. He had a knowing of the practical. He had a knowing that something good, something of great value would come from his practical actions.

Chris Sauder symbolized "the many" from Arimathea in our lives. She served in practical ways with meals, notes, and kindness. She represents the many who did things large and small, noticeable or more-often-than-not, the unnoticeable and behind the scenes. She made mention of our strengths, overlooked our weaknesses, and this despite not always being part of a more intimate circle of sharing.

In times of prolonged difficulty and stress, there is this struggle of how best to adequately share intimately beyond a few. It was work enough just to survive the day, let alone keeping all ones' friends and family in-the-know.

She represents the many who stayed in the fringes and did

so with ever-so watchful attention, looking for ways to provide practical care. To those who helped, we could never say thanks enough. I remember our trying to return the favor once to Chris. Kathy made a meal for her after the birth of their fourth child. As I was carrying this wonderfully prepared vegetable casserole meal with all the fixins up the sidewalk to their house, the bottom gave out.

I'm forever mindful that this happened despite Kathy implicit telling me to hold the bottom of the box. The deliciously prepared meal went splattering all over the sidewalk and grass. It was all for naught... Sandwiches were bought at a shop just up the street for a quick remedy to a somewhat embarrassing, yet humorous situation. Chris and her husband Joey claim they see evidence of veggie-type sproutings in their lawn each spring.

At Molly's birth, it was Chris and Dawn Beitzel gathering people to make and then hang the welcome home banner. After Molly's death, it was Chris and Ann Dienner that gathered friends to plant a special "Molly tree" on our property. They chose a beautiful weeping cherry tree. Unbeknownst to them, this particular tree traces its origins back to Japan.

In writing down Molly's stories, much of the early detail came from Kathy's journaling. And as I should have expected, there inside the front cover of her notebook was the date March 1994 and a hand-written, taped note from Chris:

My dear Kathy, since Molly's birth I have been looking for a special book for you. Please consider keeping a journal ...some of

130

the details (can) get lost over time and I know they are a blessing later.

The story of Anna also was a story of service. Scripture tells us she was married just seven years, her husband died and then she gave herself to the service of the house of Lord for most likely another sixty years. She obviously refused to be bitter and had worked through her loss, grief, and disappointment. Luke chapter 2 says she gave herself to prayer and fasting. To give oneself for that many years to service in the house of the Lord, Anna assuredly knew her place of grace and calling. Her service was to pray and to believe for the coming of the promised Messiah. Did she know and understand the whole picture? Probably not. She did what she knew to be true and left the results to God.

It seemed too as if Molly had discovered her calling. She was most content in the house of the Lord. Wherever worship was, her heart was there. She made it a canopy of worship. She seemed not to enjoy being out and about with large crowds. She liked intimacy of attention. There was little outward response at either the eighteenth birthday concert or the India concert much to others' dismay.

When one finds their calling and purpose there is an aroma of grace to do the ordinary well. Joseph of Arimathea, Chris, Anna, Molly all seemed willing to do their part without needing to know or understand the bigger picture.

Molly just being in a wheelchair seemed to draw attention, but it became more than just the wheelchair. There was this special sweet aroma that would bring others near. She seemed most comfortable at our country church in the cedars located on the outskirts and northwest side of Elizabethtown. It was the church plant that eventually evolved out of a willingness to step out of our comfort zone in 2005 to see what church planting was about. For Molly, it became a good fit. The little children would come right over to say "hi" in hopes for a returned smile. Or perhaps it was the squeeze of her hand, as Eloise Lao would do routinely.

During prayer time people seemed to always gather around Molly. She was well loved. Dreams about Molly were commonplace; words of encouragement arrived often. Songs were written about Molly, in sermons she was preached about... She was the poster child for the ever-present desire and battle cry for revival. The region was and still is filled with prayer meetings and gatherings calling in the next move of God. Surely it seemed she fit right into this next great awakening. She was the symbol of the yet-to-be-seen miraculous that we all yearned for.

In January 2018, a brother who rarely shares publicly asked permission to share what the Lord put in his heart regarding Molly. With humility and great courage he stood at the front of the church and read the message the Lord gave him to the congregation. The overriding theme was this: "Molly, I have need of you."

In the moment it could have been interpreted that now is the time for Molly to rise, shine, and get out of the wheelchair. Or it could have been taken literally as in Molly Heaven awaits your presence. The message was given in such a grace-filled way that it simply left us with words to pray about and discern. Most of us hoped for the prior but when she did breathe her last, "Molly, I have need of you" was immediately remembered.

It was literal. Jesus was calling her home.

Molly defined the aroma of contentment in one's calling.

Molly surrounded by her siblings at Joe and Angela's wedding in 2017

Hess family at Matthew and Carissa's wedding in 2018

Written by E. Daniel Martin
September 2018

The handicap ramp with white railing stands out in sharp contrast to the brown stained siding of the little church in the wildwood known as LifeGate. The ramp signals to all that "Whatever your state of ability or disability, we're here to assist you into the presence of God."

Every Sunday morning Don Hess cheerfully and lovingly propelled his invalid daughter, Molly, up that ramp in her wheel chair. Invariably those gathering in the sanctuary, having entered by the main door, would catch a glimpse through the window of the father and daughter ascending the ramp. Then there would be a wild, while attempting to be dignified, rush to be the one to open the locked door at the top of the ramp.

The fortunate one would swing the door wide open and would be the first to receive the big, grateful smile of the father and the daughter. And the father would always say for the both of them, in that the daughter couldn't speak, "Good morning," with a strong emphasis on the first word of the greeting. And the daughter would continue to smile into her father's eyes as he stroked her arm, reassuringly and protectively, as he wheeled her into the sanctuary.

Then at a very deep level of awareness, all of those gathering suddenly sensed that we had not so much welcomed and ushered one with a disability into God's presence; but rather, we ourselves had been ushered into God's presence by this one with disability. In fact, Jesus did say, "In as much as you welcome one of these little ones in my name you are welcoming me" (Matt. 18:5).

And the glory of God would, once again, descend upon us all.

CHAPTER 17

A ROOT OUT OF DRY GROUND

Through the years, bedtime with Molly had been quite the ordeal for Kathy and I; much more so for Kathy. There wasn't the luxury of simply falling asleep when one got tired. Each night, Kathy would start her bedtime tube-feeding about an hour before she hoped to go to bed. This involved pouring one and a half cans of formula into a drip bag—and trying not to spill. It involved remembering to start the pump of which we both would forget too many times to count. Adding to the liquid formula was specified and precise medicines, and then the forty-five-minute wait for the drip-bag to empty.

My routine was reduced to the simple task of taking care of Molly's suctioning, brushing her teeth, and then wheeling her from our bathroom to her bedroom. Her wheelchair would get placed at the same right angle by her bed.

Kathy always had her bed perfectly made. It was always tidied and taut. First I would roll open the covers, then tilt her wheelchair back, gather my arms around Molly, my left arm I placed around her neck and my right hand slipped under both knees, and I would slowly lift Molly up and out of her wheelchair to lay her into her comfortable bed. This same routine was done for nearly twenty-five years. That's about nine thousand times, if you're counting. Feeding her four-to-five times every day makes those totals at forty thousand or more…you get the picture. It became quite a natural routine.

There were also times when I would simply forget to pull back the bed cover sheet and would go to lift Molly over to the bed and suddenly realize my mistake, and Molly would flash a smile knowing I had to set her back down in the wheelchair to pull back the covers and sheet and then start over again. It was moments like these, whether forgotten pumps or unpulled-back sheets, that would remind us again and again that she was present, mindful of what was taking place. She understood. She was a person. She was aware of her surroundings.

Especially the last few years, as I would slowly ease and lift her up into my arms and out of the wheelchair then gently lower her into bed, I sensed the overwhelming presence and approval of the Father. It felt like a holy moment. It was a knowing that I graced in my arms an anointed and cherished daughter of Heaven…

One who was being prepared for Heaven. One highly beheld.

One highly beloved.

I sensed the whispered pleasure of the Father.

Bedtime was worship time. The music was playing at a low volume, and Molly would offer up to heaven her sacrifice of praise, her heart song, as we left her to the quietness of the night. It seemed her favorite time of day.

Within fifteen-to-twenty minutes she was fast asleep.

Night after night. Year after year.

These are the things we did because we loved, because we held fast to one who beheld great value.

For Kathy and I, our children, our extended family, her nurses Sarah and Lisha...we all say it was an honor and privilege to serve and care for Molly.

There are new seasons ahead for all of us. We look back but for a moment to see and hear what the Lord has done. We look ahead fully knowing that God will carry us through any circumstance or challenge this world might try to hurl our way.

He is able.

He knows the beginning from the end.

He can be trusted.

No doubt the disciples had a rash of varied emotion as they watched Jesus ascending up into the clouds. They would spend a lifetime realizing, pondering, and writing about the importance of his death, resurrection, and return to the right hand of the Father.

We too look up. We wonder why Jesus didn't stick around a

few more years to testify to the masses after His glorious Sunday morning resurrection. Think of the crowds! Think of the impact! Think of the crowds Molly could've attracted had she just stayed on earth as one healed.

We are left looking up wondering why God chooses us to carry on His message when knowing full well Jesus and Molly could have done it far better than us.

Yet I trust Him. Yet I dare say He knows what He is doing. He chose us. He believes in us.

Isaiah 49:16 says, "Behold, I have engraved you on the palms of my hands."

My prayer and belief is that great acts of faith will follow those who take up Molly's mantle of worship, faith, and simple trust.

These two things I ask of the Lord: that Molly's story will draw people to know the Heavenly Father, and that her story will be remembered and told to the generations to come.

As I was wrapping up the writing and editing of Molly's stories, we were privileged to host P.C. Alexander in our home. He came from India to be a part of a fundraising banquet in our area. As we shared past and present stories over a meal, he recalled our luncheon with Nicole C. Mullen the day after the concert in New Delhi. His spirit too was deeply touched over the mention of a desired worship event in Japan. And he graciously asked if he could be a part of the event when indeed it takes place.

My heart leaped. Could it be possible for churches to be born out of this Japan event? Isaiah prophesied seven hundred years before it came to pass, "like a root out of dry ground" (Isaiah 53:2).

Our twenty-four years of seemingly dry ground is worth it all if fruit comes forth. It gives new meaning, new purpose to dry ground. What if we apply faith to our dry season and believe for fruitfulness to burst forth in due season? Let's dare believe that dry grounds can and will produce a harvest of righteousness, a harvest of fruitfulness, a harvest of souls.

And so we choose to worship each day, everyday...

...until we see Him face-to-face

...until we behold Him in all His glory.

Molly is now listed among that special group called the "great cloud of witnesses" (Heb. 12:1). She is cheering and peering from the balcony of Heaven waiting for veiled curtains to open, for stages to be set.

I can only imagine...

Molly singing.

I can only imagine...

Molly now leading the choirs of Heaven.

Molly, you were a gem worth finding, a precious stone worth shining. We are forever grateful to be among the chosen few to help uncover your treasured value. You were placed on the world's stage for others to see. Thank you for allowing us to show your value to the world.

Her name means anointing.

She had it.

We experienced it.

He is worthy.

Molly, we miss you.

We'll see you someday soon.

May your Redeemer live in and through us.

May He find us faithful.

Thank you, Molly, for defining life.

A PAUSE IN PARAGUAY

One of the perks of Molly and the move to the larger house was the opportunity to accommodate and be a part of large gatherings. One such planned gathering took place in December of 2015. About twenty-five leaders from our network of churches came together on a Saturday evening. Mel and Rosemary Weaver came to our network meeting and brought along Eloise Gwinn, missionary to Paraguay and a sister to Rosemary. Eloise opened her heart to a group she did not know. Hers was a story of hope, vision, promise, and pain. Her husband Richard's focused vision of building a mission training school to reach out to the unreached parts of the world was years in the making. The vision itself encompassed student and teacher dormitories, a library, classrooms, a cafeteria, a multi-purpose worship center, and guest housing. It was fruitful and was becoming a truly remarkable campus nestled in the mountains on thirty acres near the small town of Escobar in southern Paraguay. In the midst of virtual completion, Richard died of a sudden hospital complication. Heartbroken but determined to move on, Eloise was appealing for guidance.

Around the same time Eloise shared her story, my father, age eighty-eight at the time, had completed his memoirs of his father, my grandfather. These were told and written down by my sister Sue and compiled into book form. I was only two years old when he died, and thus I never really knew him. In discussing the stories about my grandfather, my dad mentioned his father's involvement in aiding financially a particular group of thirty-five hundred refugees who were stuck in Berlin, Germany, in 1945.

In the throes of WWI, Russian Mennonites had lost everything. Some made it out in the 1920s and 1930s. When WWII was nearing an end, a destitute band of these leftover vagabonds traveled over a thousand miles on foot from Russia to Germany thinking Germany would win the war. The Germans lost. They had no place to go and lived in abandoned and makeshift housing in Berlin. But their storied plight reached the Mennonite communities in America and although there was nearly two hundred years of separation between the groups, the Holy Spirit moved upon the hearts of many in significant ways to pave the way for these refugees to find midnight-hour-type passage by train from Berlin to Holland, and from Holland to Paraguay aboard the good ship Volendam.

For some reason I pressed further and asked my dad if he remembered the giving amount; he did. I ran the numbers comparative to today's value and it was a "wow" moment as I realized this was no ordinary giving. The Holy Spirit must have really touched my grandfather, who in my then late-to the-game opinion, was a person more filled with staunch religion than filled with Holy Spirit directed living. I was glad to be wrong. This was alabaster-type giving.

It struck me then and still does now the parallel timing of hearing both my father telling his father's stories and Eloise's stories. And it was rather uncanny to find out that my grandfather's financial involvement was exactly seventy years prior! The seventy years seemed to add a touch of biblical significance, and so when the opportunity presented itself a few months later, I was compelled to go.

As of this writing, this is my third trip, and each time I go there I have increased awareness of walking in generational blessings. Many are now prospering. Streams are coming forth from a once dry and barren land. I have no doubt that many of these grandchildren and great-grandchildren of the Berlin 3500 will be a part of Eloise and Richard's vision of sending out and supporting missionaries to the unreached. The America Latina Misiones Al-mundo (ALMA) plans to open for training in March 2020.

Weaving and joining threads through the generations as only the Lord could do is a new ALMA board member; Lolita Harder. Her father as a child was part of the entourage that came from Berlin.

Richard's body was laid to rest, not in America, his place of birth, but rather on the campus that he gave birth to. Death brings resurrection. A seed planted in the ground will flourish once again. Richard and Eloise gave their all, in Richards's case, even unto death. Eloise chooses to live right next door to the campus rather than returning to her native homeland. This is home. This is where she wants to be, and I am writing much of Molly's story from this very campus.

Quite a surprise awaited us when we took a four-day trip north to the Chaco. I had all but wrapped up writing down all the stories I could remember about Molly. Prior trips had led some in our network to a church in Filadelfia, Paraguay which is about seven hours north of the campus. It is an area known as the Chaco, previously known as the Green Hell. Numerous Russian Mennonite groups established settlements there, including the Neuland group from Berlin 1945.

I had seen a family picture of a pastor and his wife and daughter from this region given to me by E. Daniel Martin. I remembered the picture because of seeing the daughter in a wheelchair and instantly had a desire to be there someday and had this desire to share Molly's story if ever given the chance.

The chance came. When they heard we were coming, the pastor asked me to share our story in the Sunday morning service. I sensed the presence of the Lord during worship and it was hardly a coincidence that they played one of our favorite songs, "Do it Again," which we had used at Molly's memorial service just six months prior. For some reason, I could not hold back the tears when their daughter Felicia was wheeled into the sanctuary during worship time.

I shared in detail Molly's story, about our connection to the song "Redeemer" and her concert in Elizabethtown and then in

New Delhi, India. It seemed well received and the pastor asked us to come back to their house that Sunday evening.

It was one of those set-ups by the Lord. For nearly three hours we were held spellbound by their stories. They told us about their walk of faith, the special move of grace in the 1990s, of salvations and miracles taking place, the start of a church and their journey as a family. He has dealt with the effects of polio since age two, their difficulties with having children, their losing two children in the third trimester. They would be married twelve years before Felicia was born. She lived despite being five weeks premature but had issues related to cerebral palsy as a result.

Felicia had uncanny resemblances and similarities to Molly... only she could talk! Kathy and I were amazed at their similarities. Both had similar mannerisms; both spent their days in a wheelchair. Both had to be fully cared for by their mothers and others. Both had strong aversions to sudden noises. Both had muscle discomforts and contortions.

But the joy-filled difference was that Felicia could talk, and she opened up deeper understanding for us about Molly and what she most likely experienced. Together the family has persevered through the years. The parents prayed for the Lord to be with and to be near Felicia. As she got older, they kept encouraging Felicia to pray and ask the Lord herself for help. And she did.

It began early for Felicia, at the age of five. Jesus would come to Felicia often and would take her on journeys. Over the years, she went on many trips throughout heaven. He would take her to view the galaxies of the universe. He loved spending time with her.

Felicia said that the Lord was with her most when times were darkest. He would hold her hand. Felicia would go on to describe the vastness and uniqueness of heaven. She would describe seeing Moses in all his prince-like regality and recalling Elisha with his bald head made her laugh out loud.

Some things she could share, and others she could not. She saw her two brothers who preceded her to heaven. One resembled her dad, the other her mom. And much to her dad's delight, Felicia exclaimed that Jesus's voice sounds just like her dad's!

A self-proclaimed lover and delighted follower of Jesus, Felicia said she would much rather be in her room talking to Jesus, that talking with people just wasn't the same. Even during our three short hours together, she seemed to disappear for moments and the assumption was she went to talk to Jesus. Felicia's stories were encouraging and refreshing to our soul. It touched us deep in our spirits.

In her young adult life, she would be called upon to pray for others. A missionary family that was transitioning from assignments in China to Kyrgyzstan asked for prayer on what city to set up as home base. As Felicia was praying, the Lord journeyed her to the actual country and suggested to her the city and the very house they should consider moving to! She was excited to pass along the visitation to the missionary friends.

It was LifeGate's pastor, Don Lamb, that said it well at Molly's memorial, "In between the many smiling pictures of Molly there was a lot of work...a lot of pain."

This family would state the same. It was not easy, yet the Lord takes and makes up for our weaknesses. He ordains that a special grace follows the least of these.

We feasted on some Brazilian-branded ham and pineapple cheese-crusted pizza while the stories continued. It all resonated with us. It felt like we were on the Emmaus road experiencing what the disciples went through as it was recorded, "Did not our hearts burn within us while He talked with us..." (Luke 24:32).

As a teenager, Jesus took Felicia to southern Israel in the Negev desert...just to teach her to dance. The angels cleared an area and spread their wings to give them shade. And arm in arm they danced.

Her stories paralleled what we believed to be Molly's journey. Though Molly could never tell us, it was something we and others sensed was happening.

Recalling Kathy's words at Molly's graveside service...

I am convinced that you walked and talked with Jesus and fell asleep to the voices of angels singing over you. Because you did not speak in this world, you weren't distracted by your own commentary, and it seemed you were tuned in to the heartbeat of heaven. You were a faithful prayer warrior, and we would ask you to pray with us for specific things dear to our hearts.

Our trip to northern Paraguay was the perfect closure to writing down Molly's stories. It reaffirmed our belief that when Molly was weak, He was strong. It affirmed to us that heaven is present with those who have childlike faith, that heaven becomes real to those who lack.

Upon our return home, I got wind of another uncanny connection. It made me smile. Nicole C. Mullen was just returning from ten days in southern Israel. She, along with Kathy Lee Gifford, were filming and producing in the Negev Desert a new song and oratory story titled "The God Who Sees." I would not be surprised to find out someday that the filming took place in the same location where Jesus taught Felicia to dance. That's our God.

Learning the story of my grandfather's giving and Eloise coming to our house gave me the initial spark of interest to go to Paraguay. Now returning for a third trip, and this time with Kathy, it seemed a blessing beyond measure.

May we live mindful of the faithfulness of others and the faith of those before us as it has generational impact. There are chapters yet to be written about those who will be inspired by the life, worship, and prayers of Molly Hess. Joseph and Angela, Kalah and Matt, Emily and Seth, Matthew and Carissa all have unwritten chapters. So do the grandchildren to date: Jake and Landon, Lucas and Ben, and Cameron Lynn.

To those yet born, to those in Elizabethtown, to those in India, Paraguay, and beyond, this I know and believe: Molly's stories will continue to inspire many.

Molly defined generational blessings.

SEND A NOTE

We would love to hear from you. Send us your thoughts and messages via email to **unrequestedblessings@gmail.com**. Visit us online at **www.unrequestedblessings.com**.

DON HESS'S MEMORIAL MESSAGE

August 8, 2018

We are and have been surrounded by communities of faith, hope, and a future. Kathy and I and our children are here today to say thanks. Molly could not have changed so many lives without your giving us love, care, and kindness. It's been so deep, so rich, so real...

I want to thank the Worship Center for opening up their facilities to us today. Our journey began next door in what was then just a warehouse. Many of you here today have been with us from Molly's day one. Monday night we as a family watched Molly's baby dedication on home video. Pastor Sam, as he has done so well for the last forty years, was speaking words of life over Molly from the very beginning.

For our fifteenth wedding anniversary, friends and family who I guess thought we looked a little worn out, sent Kathy and I on a cruise. It's not so easy when you have five children between the ages of two and eleven, with Molly being four at that time. We saw potential in a young couple and asked them to live at our house and care for the children for eight days. That couple was Matt and Kelly Mylin. I guess it was the test to see if they could handle pastoring the Worship Center someday.

A special thank you to those watching via live stream in Kansas, Virginia, North Carolina, Texas, Colorado, Germany, Barbados,

Ethiopia, and India.

Molly, without ever saying a word, has touched lives around the world.

When Molly was eleven or twelve, the song "Redeemer" was introduced to Molly by Kathy, and it forever changed our lives. I should have known some challenges still might be ahead as the song comes from the book of Job chapter 19 verse 25, "I know that my Redeemer lives, and in the end He will stand on the Earth."

With Molly, she responded with great effort to sing along. No words, just sounds coming from somewhere deep within her spirit. Romans 8:26 refers to the Holy Spirit helping our weaknesses and using these utterances to bring forth the will of God in this earth. Molly's worship moved our hearts, it moved the Father's heart, and things began to shake and shift here on earth, sometimes beyond our liking and beyond our control.

Nicole C. Mullen wrote us a note this week saying Molly "now knows our Redeemer in ways that we can only dream about!"

I wonder sometimes if Nicole would have ever written the song "Redeemer" had it not been for some hard times? That one song affected Molly, affected our region, affected India, and now is the vision for a three-city 2020 Japan tour with Nicole and the Kawase family. I will continue. We will go and we will do because of Molly. Because she liked her music. Because she knew her Redeemer lived, because others need to know.

By the end of the book, Job comes to realize his smallness compared to God's greatness. Who but He can tell the sun where to stand in the morning? It is He who tells the oceans you can only come this far (Job 38:11-12).

Our questioning God as to whether He is good and just in ours or others' circumstances puts us on the throne. Then we become the judge as to what we deem fair. And that, we have experienced, is not a place we want to be. Let's not go down the path of disappointment in God. Let's not get so consumed with the how, why, and who did us wrong. Rather let's consume ourselves with how we can respond with words of faith and hope.

Two Sundays ago, late at night, just as I was leaving the hospital, leaving David Kandole at Molly's bedside, Calvin Greiner called me. Calvin could barely get the words out, but he kept saying, "Jesus is so close with Molly. He is right there. Right now. He is so close. He is with her."

Friday just over a week ago, I was by Molly's bedside at two thirty in the afternoon. I dozed off for about ten minutes and awoke out of a fog to a young girl saying in such a light-hearted and carefree way, "I am going to remember this day for as long as I live." I looked around. Molly was still in bed hooked up to the ventilator. I checked my iPad to look at the last few songs that were being played to see if somehow that phrase was part of a song that played. There was none. It was a beautiful carefree voice with no sense of awareness of tubes, oblivious to discomfort, no wince or waver in her voice... It had to be Molly. There is no other explanation. She was free on Friday. On the early morning hours of Monday, August 6, her heart on earth stopped beating. But Molly's heart for her brothers and sisters, her mom and dad, and for each one of you here today, forever beats again."

KATHY HESS'S MESSAGE, SPOKEN AT MOLLY'S GRAVESIDE

August 12, 2018

Molly, you had a strong will to live and to enjoy life despite all your challenges. We all thrilled over your smiles and laughter over the years. I was always impressed with, and blessed by, your peaceful spirit (as opposed to the agitation and unrest I noticed in other children with similar disabilities). Although you needed to be left on the sidelines at times, you were mostly with us through all the family activities and events, and you loved being right in the middle of all the commotion.

I am convinced that you walked and talked with Jesus and fell asleep to the voices of angels singing over you. Because you did not speak in this world, you weren't distracted by your own commentary, and it seemed you were tuned in to the heartbeat of heaven. You were a faithful prayer warrior, and we would ask you to pray with us for specific things dear to our hearts.

Molly, you kept alive our desire for the miraculous, and to press in to knowing God more fully. You were a gift I didn't always know how to receive, but you were a constant reminder to me of how precious and valuable life is, and to never let go of hope.

Molly, you were loved well by each of your brothers and sisters; and I know that you loved and treasured each one also. For your twenty-four-and-a-half years with us, I am grateful…

JOSEPH'S MEMORIAL MESSAGE

(Molly's brother)

I feel totally inadequate to the task of finding words that would do justice to Molly's life. Attempting to appropriately describe the person that represented so much of what was beautiful and so much of what was painful about life meant to me and to our family is a task that's simply impossible. There are so many things about her life that we probably won't know until we get to heaven, so instead of speculating about answers I don't have, I'll talk about two things know for certain:

1) In many ways, Molly defined our family.

I'm ashamed to admit that for many years we as a family and I personally fought that definition believing it to be a negative characterization. Don't get me wrong, I loved Molly and felt deeply for her, but her physical challenges made certain things a lot more difficult for our family. They radically changed the responsibilities thrust on my parents. They made it more difficult to go out to eat or on family vacations. It was sometimes embarrassing to sit in church or go out in public because she would attract attention. In my mind the goal was always to minimize the impact she had on our lives—that somehow making sure we had a "normal" life was the best alternative available. It took several years, but by the time she was a teenager we started to recognize that in many ways—in arguably the most important ways—she defined us as a family... but far from being a bad thing, we realized how blessed we are that she did. Molly gave our family the ability to rally together, to spend more time with one another, to confront the difficulties of life and be better prepared for the challenges to our faith. We saw firsthand from our parents how one reacts to suffering. How a mother and father support one another in the tough times. And I'd like to think we siblings were examples to one another. I can't tell you how much joy it brings me remembering so clearly Molly sitting by the piano, smiling while Kalah practiced her lessons. Or Emily dancing with her in her wheelchair in the kitchen. Or Matthew crawling over her as a baby. She brought so much joy to our home. And it is a privilege to be defined by someone so special.

2) For someone who never spoke a word, Molly was a great teacher.

She taught me perspective: whatever struggles I was going through seemed so much smaller after considering hers.

She taught me patience: waiting on God's timing took on new meaning in light of her waiting for her new body.

She taught me the power of observation: observation is really all Molly had—observing how other people interacted with her taught me a lot about human nature and the capacity for making the best of a difficult situation.

She taught me how to think: I had no choice but to wrestle with tough questions about God's goodness and purpose.

She taught me about unfairness and God's sacrificial love: Molly did nothing wrong and yet she was dealt a terrible hand in this life. I on the other hand was totally aware of my sins and yet physically and mentally healthy. That's not fair but neither was God's sacrifice of His Son. Thank God this life is unfair.

So in closing, Molly, if you're listening I want you to know it was an honor having you as a sister these past twenty-four years. Thank you for defining our family and teaching us a little bit about the nature of God. Not a single one of us would be the people that we are now as adults if it weren't for your profound impact on our lives—and I'm struck by how few individuals have had the ability to make that profound an impact on those around them like you have in your relatively short time with us. I don't know how many years it will be until we meet again, but I know it will be a glorious reunion. I love you.

EMILY'S MEMORIAL MESSAGE

(Molly's sister)

From a young age I remember having the desire to help take care of Molly, carry her around and help hold her feeding tube. I'm sure there were times during those young years I wondered why Molly was different than other babies. However, I don't have those memories and I attribute that to my parents for always making us kids all feel loved and cared for equally.

For this reason, I didn't think Molly was different or that our family was different. As I got older I remember praying a lot for Molly's healing but looking back these were more selfish prayers—I wanted her healed so I could play dress-up and sports with her and hear about her day and her interests.

Some of my favorite memories were when everyone in the family was away and it was just Molly and I at home. I'd crawl in bed with her and tell her about my day and the middle school drama I was going through. I'd write in my journals about wanting so badly to hear Molly respond back and wanting to have that big sister role of giving her advice and caring for her needs.

As I got older and was out of the house more often, I'd make a point to spend time with Molly when I was home in the evenings. I'd turn on music and we'd dance together in the kitchen, and I'd play with her hair and rub her feet. I wanted her to know how much I loved her because I would have this guilty feeling that she might get lonely as we all started getting older and moved out of the house. Looking back I am certain that she was never alone as God always had his angels with her.

In addition to praying for Molly's healing, I remember having dreams of her being healed—the most vivid one was several years ago, which I shared in the India video. In it, Molly was on a stage in front of thousands of people and I was peeking around the curtain with the biggest smile because I finally got the chance to be on the sidelines cheering her on like she had done for us all through our sports careers and other accomplishments. In hindsight, I believe that dream came true as demonstrated by her experiences with Nicole C. Mullen here in Pennsylvania and in India when she was on that stage. What a proud sister I am of those opportunities, and I was ready for more of them and wasn't ready for her to go.

In closing, I also strongly believe that God had need of her. None of us know when it is our time. Despite the pain we are feeling now, I cannot deny her the joy she is experiencing as she dances and runs through fields of wildflowers and sings in that heavenly choir. Right now she's sitting at the table with Jesus eating real food for the first time in her life. These images give me such joy. I think all our prayers are that God continues to give us dreams and visions and in them we can see glimpses of Molly experiencing all of this. In doing so, it makes Heaven so much more real, which reminds us that this is not our home and soon we will be home with Molly.

KALAH'S MEMORIAL MESSAGE

(Molly's sister)

When I was young and would introduce friends to Molly, I would always follow-up with the sentence, "We believe that God is going to heal her one day." That was what each member of my family firmly believed. Even before Molly was born, prophecies were spoken over her life. As she grew, people would say things like, "Molly sees angels" and God wanted to heal her." We clung to those words as we watched her deal with pain and operate in a body that barely functioned. And we cried out for God to fulfill these promises.

A while back, God spoke to me and said, "Will you still declare my goodness, even if your sister is not healed?" At that moment I realized how much of my faith was tied up in when God heals her, then I will proclaim His goodness. How many of us get caught up in the even ifs? Will you declare His goodness, even if… that one thing that you most want to happen, never happens?

I grieve because I miss Molly, and I am sad that I did not witness her physical healing. Yet God did keep His promise, Molly is healthy and whole with her Creator in heaven. She is experiencing the ultimate fulfillment and joy. No more pain. No more hindrances. Just freedom to talk, sing, run, and dance.

I am thankful for the twenty-four years' worth of memories she made on this earth. The impact she had on so many. I am thankful to be her sister, journeying through life with her, and I am thankful that she is in a better place. I long for the day that I will see her again.

Thank you all for loving her, and I hope that you'll share of God's goodness every time you mention her name.

WRITTEN BY MATT, MOLLY'S YOUNGER BROTHER TWELVE DAYS PRIOR TO HER PASSING

July 26, 2018

Dear Molly,

I've been thinking a lot about you this week. In fact, there are a lot of thoughts I have about you that I'd like to pass on. There is a lot emotion as I'm typing this. So if you don't mind, I'll just write down what I can put into words. Truthfully, this letter might be mostly for my own benefit, but I want you to hear these words, and I want you to know how loved you are. Mom and Dad tell me there is a good chance they are going to do a tracheotomy in order to help you breathe better. I'm confident that if this is true, it's just another obstacle and setback that God is going to give you the strength to overcome. You've always been a fighter Molly.

Growing up, I never really had the chance, or maybe even the awareness, to be angry about your situation. For as long as I've been alive, it is all I've known, and it's just the way it was. Even if I did have the chance to be upset, there were three older siblings ahead of us that I watched and I never saw them be angry or upset about your condition. Sure, there were times where I wanted to know why you had to be in a wheelchair. And there were even times where I remember wondering why our family pictures didn't look like other families' pictures. Or why we had to make sure a place was handicap accessible before going there as a family. I feel guilty even thinking about those memories Molly, but I'm just being honest. Mom and Dad always did an unbelievable job of taking care of you while also taking care of the rest of the kids and making everything feel "normal." They never let us feel like our childhood was "different" by any means. It really is a credit to them and the older siblings that I never felt the need to question God or get upset that you were born with cerebral palsy. They did such a good job of explaining God's goodness. I still trust in God's plan for your life and my trust in God will never waver. I fully believe in His goodness, and I fully believe He loves you more than I can understand. I know that His thoughts are higher than our thoughts and His ways are greater than our ways.

But that doesn't stop the emotion that wells up inside of me every time I talk about you Molly. Since somewhere around my high school years and the time I started college, I haven't been able to say your name in a context that is deeper than surface level without starting to cry. Even thinking about your life when I'm by myself automatically brings tears to my eyes. For this reason, even though it sounds selfish, I try to suppress those emotions before they start. I'll play it off or change the subject or keep my prayers to God about you relatively short. It hasn't been hard for me to play it off because I was used to doing that exact thing all my life. "It is what it is. God has a plan for her life. I love her." I didn't interact with too many people that didn't already know your condition anyway.

The truth is that as I'm writing this, I'm tired of suppressing the emotion that is inside of me. I know God has a plan for your life Molly but that doesn't change the fact that I get angry about it. I get angry because it isn't fair. I get angry because you didn't get to choose this life. I get angry because it should be me that's never been able to walk or talk. If someone has to be in a wheelchair then I wish it was me. You've done your time. You deserve the chance to experience life like the rest of us. You deserve to play sports and go hiking and walk down the aisle someday. I didn't choose my life either, so it's not fair that I'm where I am and you might have to get a trach just to continue breathing. I think that's where most of my emotion comes from Molly. I want to know why it couldn't have been me instead. It just doesn't seem right. And it also doesn't sit well that God didn't even give you a voice so that you could complain or speak up about it or defend yourself. When I reflect on my own life, I've made mistakes and it would at least make sense for me to be punished. But what have you ever done? All you have done is sit there and smile despite it all.

Now Molly, I know God is in control of your life, and I know He is so good. What I really want to tell you is that I can't wait to see you physically whole. I know God is going to continue using you to reach countless more people in whatever way He sees fit. You have already impacted more people than you even know. And it would only be silly to think your physical conditions could limit how God plans to use you in the future. But I want you to know that I think about and look forward to the day that we'll get to dance together, shoot hoops together, and play card games together. I just don't know if that day will be on this earth or if we'll have to wait until heaven.

I admire you. I respect you. And I love you so much Molly. Thank you for bringing so much joy to our family and for bringing so much hope to this world. Remember that you are an inspiration to so many, including your little bro.

Love, Matt

DISCOGRAPHY

"Blessings," Laura Story, 2011, #5, *Blessings*, Laura Stories (AS-CAP), 2011. Lyrics reprinted with permission from Capital CMP Publishing.

"Sovereign Over Us," Michael Smith, 2011, Thankyou Music PRS, 2011. Partial lyrics reprinted with permission Capital CMG Publishing.

"Redeemer," Nicole C. Mullen, 1998, Word Records, 2000. Lyrics reprinted gratis with permission from artist.

"Molly's Song," Sonya Penya. Lyrics reprinted with permission from songwriter/artist Sonya Penya.

"Call On Jesus," Nicole C. Mullen, 2001, Album, #5, *Talk About It*, Word Records, 2001. Lyrics reprinted gratis with permission from artist.

"Everything," Lauren Daigle, 2018, Album, #8, Centricity Music, 12Tone Music, LLC. Lyrics reprinted with permission from Capital CMP Publishing.